DATE			

BEOWULF

A VERSE TRANSLATION

BEOWULF

A VERSE TRANSLATION

Frederick Rebsamen

IconEditions
An Imprint of HarperCollins*Publishers*

FIRST EDITION

Designed by Cassandra J. Pappas

Library of Congress Cataloging-in-Publication Data

Beowulf. English.
Beowulf : a verse translation / Frederick Rebsamen. — 1st ed.
p.   cm.
Includes bibliographical references.
ISBN 0-06-438437-3 (cloth)
1. Epic poetry, English (Old)—Modernized versions.   I. Rebsamen, Frederick R.   II. Title.
PR1583.R43   1991
829'·3—dc20   91-55103

91 92 93 94 95 AC/HC 10 9 8 7 6 5 4 3 2 1

Acknowledgments

FOR ADVICE, encouragement, and criticism, my grateful thanks to the following:

To Fred Robinson for telling me that, in constant search of the right words, I was neglecting certain matters of quantity and secondary stress. Though I have not been able to consistently capture all of the Old English forms after much revision of the manuscript, this translation is now much better than it might have been without that warning, and *Beowulf* scholars will note how I have profited by Fred's intelligent essays clarifying several disputed passages.

To Dick Ringler and the five students in his *Beowulf* study group for spending an entire afternoon comparing a sample of my work with the original, an uncommonly generous response to my request for Dick's esteemed opinion of the translation, and for the fine encouragement of this perceptive group, which has given me a chronic boost.

To Joe Tuso, whose critical edition of *Beowulf* reflects his long acquaintance with the poem, for understanding what I have tried to do and for giving me the kind of strong and informed approval that every writer cherishes.

To my editor, Cass Canfield, Jr., who rightly rejected an earlier draft of this translation in a kind, encouraging letter and then asked to see it again when he learned that I had completely revised it, displaying an editorial concern exceedingly rare today and leading us both to this happy conclusion.

Especially to L. D. Clark, longtime friend and ruthless critic, who spent too many hours applying the skills of his acclaimed scholarly writing to three early drafts of the introduction and keeping me from making all kinds of silly mistakes—then giving praise to the poetry at a time when I needed it, along with unflagging encouragement from the first day of work to the last.

Finally, the greatest debt of all, to the anonymous poet who created this wonderfully conceived work of early medieval imagination and wrapped it in such ringing verses that I heartily wish all students of English literature could read it in the language in which he composed it. I find that I cannot improve upon my dedication of an earlier book on *Beowulf:* "To the poet, whoever he was, whose song gave a richer light to that first bright flare of English civilization, this book is gratefully dedicated."

Introduction

 In 1936, J. R. R. Tolkien delivered a lecture before members of the British Academy entitled "*Beowulf:* The Monsters and the Critics." The wisdom and eloquence of this lecture finally delivered *Beowulf* from historians, archaeologists, mythologists, linguists—the list is long. Conceding that students of all these disciplines can find much to ponder there, he said, however, that "it is plainly only in the consideration of *Beowulf* as a poem, with an inherent poetic significance, that any view or conviction can be reached or steadily held," and further remarked that "*Beowulf* is in fact so interesting as poetry, in places poetry so powerful, that this quite overshadows the historical content, and is largely independent even of the most important facts . . . that research has discovered."

In this translation of *Beowulf*—the only translation I am aware of that attempts throughout to imitate the Old English poetic form as closely as is practical in Modern English—I have tried to respect those words in every line. However, because of the modern reader's unfamiliarity with ancient Germanic poetry and Anglo-Saxon history, any translation should be prefaced by a discussion of those aspects of the poem which establish a matrix for the poet's invention: the historical background, the principal characters, the structure of the poem, the dates of composition and of the manuscript, the source and importance of *Beowulf,* the poet's compromise between Christianity and paganism, and a description of the Old English poetic form, as well as a few words about Beowulf himself and the three monsters.

HISTORICAL BACKGROUND

Beowulf is a poem, a work of fiction, centered on Beowulf and his fights with monsters. Yet many historical/legendary characters and events are mentioned in the poem, and the Danes, Swedes, and Geats provide the necessary background for Beowulf's long and eventful life.

Both history and legend place the Danes and Swedes within the fifth and sixth centuries A.D., the North Germanic "Heroic Age" reflected in much of medieval Icelandic prose and poetry. The Danes lived in what is now Denmark and the southern tip of Sweden. Hrothgar, whose great hall was somewhere on the island of Zealand, is their king at the beginning of the poem, and the other members of that dynasty are accounted for in the course of the narrative. The Swedes, whose hostilities among themselves and against the Geats through three generations are featured in "installments" during the final third of the poem, lived in Sweden north of the "great lakes," Vänern and Vättern.

The identity of the Geats remains obscure, though in this poem they must have lived in Southern Sweden, between the Danes and the two lakes, a territory I have referred to as "Götland" in this translation. Gregory of Tours, who wrote his history of the Franks near the end of the sixth century, says that a king named Hygelac ("Clochilaico" in his Latin) conducted a raid in Frankish territory around the year 520. An anonymous eighth-century history of the Franks repeats this statement. So we may think of Hygelac's disastrous expedition up the Rhine, when we come to it in *Beowulf,* as having occurred around 520, and date the fictional events in the poem accordingly. Gregory and the anonymous historian identify Hygelac as a Danish king, but a third manuscript, the eighth-century *Liber Monstrorum*, written in England, says that "Huiglaucus" was king of the "Getis." Exactly who these "Getis" were, and the Geats of *Beowulf*, has never been clearly determined.

Hygelac, whose sister was Beowulf's mother, is king of the Geats at the beginning of the poem, and at the end Beowulf has replaced Hygelac's son on the throne and ruled for fifty years. Beowulf's father, Ecgtheow, was a Waegmunding, a tribe unknown outside this poem. Wiglaf, who appears at the end of the poem as Beowulf's successor, is also a Waegmunding. There is no mention of Beowulf's wife (if he had one) or any descendants.

THE PRINCIPAL CHARACTERS

Seventy-five personal names appear in *Beowulf*, along with thirty-two names of places, families, nations, and swords. I have listed sixty-five of these names in an appendix for reasons there given, but while they lend a richness to the poem that would have been appreciated by an Anglo-Saxon audience, the modern reader need be primarily concerned with only a few. Only ten characters speak, four of them of minor importance. Thus the reader may concentrate on the six important speakers—Hrothgar, his queen Wealhtheow, Unferth, Hygelac, Wiglaf, and Beowulf—and of course the three monsters.

STRUCTURE

The structure of *Beowulf* is a gratifying surprise, completely unexpected in an age which favored straightforward heroic lays concerning conflicts between human beings. It is unlike any other poem in English literature or any other Germanic literature, and Tolkien's description of *Beowulf* as a "heroic-elegiac poem" emphasizes its uniqueness.

After a genealogy of the Danes and the establishment of Hrothgar in his great new hall, we learn of the ravages of Grendel and the arrival of Beowulf to help. From these opening lines through Beowulf's fights with Grendel and Grendel's mother and his return to his homeland, the progress is "interrupted" from time to time by allusions to earlier people and events, as brief as five lines and as long as ninety-two. These compact allusions provide a shift from Beowulf's fights with monsters to the more conventional tales of conflicts among humans, and are presented as pauses in the narrative and contrasts with or reflections of Beowulf's character and his deeds. The pace is relaxed and the narrative rich in details, with entertaining interludes like Unferth's challenge and Beowulf's response, and the description of the victory feast after Grendel's death.

The final third of the poem becomes strongly elegiac, an account of Beowulf as an old man fighting his final, futile battle, the end of a long and remarkable life. Worked into this section, not in chronological order but in a natural way, are four accounts of the Geat-Swede conflicts. There are also three accounts of Hygelac's last battle, Beowulf's nostalgic reminiscences, two anonymous speeches which contain some of the most beautiful elegiac verses in English literature, the introduction of Wiglaf, and a long, foreboding speech by an anonymous "messenger" to the Geats awaiting news of Beowulf's fight with the dragon. The handling of time in this section anticipates modern literature and greatly enhances its elegiac quality.

Thus the entire poem is an account of Beowulf's fights with three monsters surrounded by and interlarded with "digressions," as they are too often called, which round out the poem and give it that rich background that so annoyed early critics who wished to have Beowulf fighting other heroes instead of monsters. It was in response to this sort of criticism that Tolkien delivered his lecture, explaining why the poem is exactly right as it is, and pointing out that the contrast between the Grendel and dragon sections is "essentially a balance, an opposition of ends and beginnings. In its simplest terms it is a contrasted description of two moments in a great life, rising and setting, an elaboration of the ancient and intensely moving contrast between youth and age, first achievement and final death."

DATE OF COMPOSITION AND OF THE MANUSCRIPT

The unique manuscript of *Beowulf,* produced about 1000 A.D., was preserved in ways unknown and eventually included in the great library of Sir Robert Cotton, who died in 1631. This manuscript, copied on vellum by two scribes, was damaged at the top and outer edges by a fire in 1731, which obscured letters and some entire words. But the Icelandic scholar Grimur Thorkelin made a copy of the manuscript in 1787, before the scorched leaves had badly crumbled, and also commissioned a professional copyist ignorant of Old English to make another copy, imitating the Old English insular script, in that same year. The importance of these two copies, and of the early editions of the poem beginning with Thorkelin's in 1815, is profound, as the reading of any page of Frederick Klaeber's edition of *Beowulf* will indicate. Though there are some uncertain readings here and there, and a few leaves are badly damaged, a good modern edition presents the poem as about 95 percent sound, a miraculous survivor of the ravages of history.

The manuscript is obviously faithful for the most part to the original composition. The rich language and innovative quality of both poetry and structure indicate that a major talent, strong enough to override the few corruptions and possible interpolations of later scribes, composed the poem pretty much as we have it.

The date of the original composition will be forever debated. In earlier years, most scholars agreed that the poem was composed at some time during the life of Bede, the great Northern English teacher, biographer, and historian who died in 735. However, the supremacy of Mercia (the English Midlands) after Bede's death, under two successive kings who dominated all of England south of the Humber River, provided the best of poets with powerful patrons, and the later eighth century is therefore favored by some as a likely period for the poem's composition. Recently an entire book and a book-length anthology of essays have been published indicating that the *Beowulf* poet may have lived at any time between the late seventh century and the early eleventh. The important question is this: When and where lived an Anglo-Saxon king with enough wealth and sophistication to sponsor such a skillful poet as this, who must have been in demand at the best of courts?

THE SOURCE AND IMPORTANCE OF BEOWULF

Anglo-Saxon England is curiously viewed by most as a place of warring primitive tribes worshiping pagan gods and dominated by illiterate kings constantly fighting among themselves and drinking the nights away while their unlettered minstrels recited tales of conquest and bloodshed, sheltering in smoky halls strewn about with bones and cracked drinking horns. This may well have been true of some kingdoms from the first arrivals of Angles, Saxons, and Jutes in England around 450 and on down through the final conquest of the Romano-Celtic inhabitants about a century later, but beginning with the Christianization of Kent in 597 and the ensuing arrival in Northumbria of Celtic Christian missionaries from Wales, Ireland, and Iona, with the establishment of monastic seats of learning under several very literate and sophisticated kings, that picture must be drastically altered.

Anglo-Saxon audiences loved to hear tales of the early North Germanic peoples like the Danes, Swedes, and Geats of the sixth century, just as we enjoy books and movies about Henry VIII and Sir Thomas More, Henry's many wives and his daughter Elizabeth and all the battles and courtly intrigues of the sixteenth century. A poem like *Beowulf*—i.e., long and leisurely, distinguished by tales of the North Germanic Heroic Age—could have been composed at any time between about 650 and the beginning of serious Danish and Norwegian invasions of England after the first third of the ninth century. Northumbria in the seventh century was ruled for a time by two kings, Oswald and his successor, Oswiu, brothers who had been well educated when young by Celtic Christian teachers on the island of Iona. Following them came another educated king, Aldfrith, whose twenty-year reign (685–705) made possible the learning, scholarship, and artistic production of Northumbrian monasteries during the Age of Bede, from the late seventh century through the first third of the eighth. During this period were produced the many fine literary works of Bede, including the first great coordinated history of the European Middle Ages, his *Ecclesiastical History of the English People*. Bede's friend Eadfrith, bishop of Lindisfarne, produced one of the most beautiful illuminated manuscripts of any period anywhere in the world, the Lindisfarne Gospels. During this same period a magnificent stone cross, now preserved at the Ruthwell Church in Dumfriesshire, Scotland, and originally standing some eighteen feet tall, was produced by a master artist, who included, along the margins on two faces of the cross, runic inscriptions which form an early Northern version of one of the finest poems in Old English, "The Dream of the Rood," in which the cross of the Crucifixion speaks, telling its marvelous story.

Immediately following this period, and covering most of the rest of the eighth century, two Mercian kings, Aethelbald and Offa, made their courts the most powerful throughout England south of the Humber, Offa being treated by Charlemagne as a friend and equal worth corresponding with. During the reign of either of these kings, *Beowulf* could have been composed. In fact, from the Age of Bede down to the Viking Age in England (an unlikely time for an English poem praising Danes), a number of kings in various areas of England held courts rich and knowledgeable enough to attract such a man as the *Beowulf* poet.

In addition to the learning and sophistication of several Anglo-

Saxon kings, an early-seventh-century cenotaph ship burial in East Anglia, known as the Sutton Hoo burial, has given us an example of the numerous treasures and exquisite artwork to be found at the court of one early king, items too rich and varied to describe here but sufficient to rank him with any king in the Germanic world. Museums throughout England contain a splendid variety of other treasures; literary descriptions and manuscript illuminations add to this picture of royal wealth. And who knows what evidence of the magnificence of Anglo-Saxon courts disappeared after the Battle of Hastings?

The Old English poetry that has survived, most of it in four great manuscripts, is almost all a blend of the old Germanic poetic form with the new Christian teaching that was first composed, according to Bede, by Caedmon in the third quarter of the seventh century. It is much earlier than any other vernacular poetry in medieval Europe and in many ways distinct from the later recorded Icelandic poetry, the only other sizable body of early Germanic poetry that has survived in manuscript. The great variety of length and subject matter of Old English poetry, the more than 30,000 lines that have come down to us, precludes any kind of summary here. It is a noble body of verse, including many poems of great beauty and strength that fully reward the effort required to learn how to read them.

It was in this tradition that the *Beowulf* poet, innovative though he was, composed his work, and we may imagine the splendor of a court wherein such a poet may have worked. The hall would be hung with rich tapestries, furnished with handsomely wrought benches and trestle tables, distinguished by a "high-seat" inlaid with ivory and burnished with gold, the king's table graced with imported glass and silverware, elaborate drinking horns and cups of precious metals and stones. The royal family and important members of the king's retinue would be richly dressed, with brooches, bracelets, necklaces, and armlets of gold and garnets. Fine hawks and dogs and horses, heirloom armor and weapons, saddles and bridles often adorned with ivory and silver, would be a part of this picture. And of course the ever-present minstrel with his harp would be there at the feet of his king, ready to recite from his large repertory when the moment was right.

In the literature of Western Europe, *Beowulf* is by far the earliest poem of such length and distinction in any vernacular language after the fall of Rome. In it we find the earliest references to heroes of such later Icelandic works as the *Völsunga Saga* and the *Hrólfs Saga Kraka*. It is a thoroughly English poem, comparable in technique, language, patristic wisdom, and beauty to shorter poems like "The Wanderer" and "The Seafarer," yet different from and greater than any other Old English poem. *Beowulf* stands at the beginning of English civilization and English poetry, "between the worlds" as R. W. Chambers said. It salutes the dying of the old and the birth of the new, and belongs to everyone whose native tongue is English.

RELIGION

The *Beowulf* poet was either a Christian or very familiar with and influenced by Christianity. The very tone of the poem in places, especially in the final third, reflects the Christian patristic influence that pervades much of Old English poetry. But some of the principal characters are historically North Germanic pagans, and much of this tradition is retained by the poet, notably in some of the characteristics of Beowulf. The poet's skill in blending these traditions is one of the most remarkable aspects of his work.

The way in which the poet solves the problem of religion in this heroic-elegiac poem composed for a Christian audience is one thing that leads me to believe that the poem was composed not long after 700. At that time, although the Anglo-Saxons were generally converted to Christianity, they were also strongly aware of their pagan past. Thus the poet, while introducing the idea of only one god, a kind of Old Testament god whose name is spelled exactly as today, does not push things further, makes no mention of Christ or anything else in the New Testament. Also the concepts of Heaven and Hell were ambivalent at that time, especially in a tale of Northern kings who lived in the distant past, and I have not capitalized these words in the translation.

Not one pagan god is ever mentioned. Although the Old English word *wyrd*, akin to Modern High German *werden* and based on a concept of "that which will happen," appears in the poem, it is used only ten times as a proper noun, and far from being the name of a god, it is rather a kind of enigmatic force—once referred to as "she"—somewhat similar to Fortune in later medieval literature. It is used twice as a verb (to injure or destroy), once as a common noun (fact or deed), and once as an adjective (destined), and it is not capitalized by any modern editor of *Beowulf*. A significant passage, referring to Grendel's abduction of one of Beowulf's men, says that Grendel would have carried off even more men "had not wise God and that man's [Beowulf's] courage withstood *wyrd*."

God, by contrast, is mentioned thirty-two times as God and at least sixty times (I have not tried to count them all) under several other names—Shaper, Wielder, Measurer, Father, Deemer, Glory-King, and Old English words now lost such as *Frea* and *Dryhten*. Though the pagan Germanic tradition is reflected in many ways, one god, named God and introduced through Christianity, is in charge.

Beowulf and the Monsters

Beowulf is obviously a creation of the poet, though partial comparisons have been made between him and somewhat similar characters in folklore and Icelandic sagas. As related to other characters in the poem, he would probably have been born shortly before 500 and died as a very old man. His "fifty-year reign" (like that of Hrothgar and Grendel's mother) is a poetic cliché.

That Beowulf's origin is obscure, that he apparently never married and/or produced any children, that he returned alone from the battle that took the life of his king instead of dying by his side in the best Germanic-heroic tradition, that he was almost entirely inactive in the Geat-Swede conflicts, that he seems at times superhuman and at other times merely a remarkable man, that he is such a curious blend of pagan and Christian (compared by some with a Christian knight), that he never appears anywhere else in all the literature of the North—these things are not bothersome or difficult to understand when we realize that a major poet was trying something big and new, and that he created for his work an original character to bring together all of its complex features.

As for the monsters, they were real enough to Anglo-Saxons ten or twelve centuries ago. Grendel and his mother were creatures of evil and darkness, feared by the Anglo-Saxons before and after conversion to Christianity, seen by Christians as descendants of Cain, God's enemies, lurking in the night outside the firelit halls. The way the poet describes these monsters, with just a few details here and there, somehow makes them more fearful and menacing than any kind of detailed portrait would have done.

The dragon is yet one more indication of the poet's originality. To quote Tolkien again: ". . . real dragons, essential both to the machinery and the ideas of a poem or tale, are actually rare. In northern literature there are only *two* that are significant." One is the third monster in *Beowulf* and the other (which is briefly referred to in *Beowulf*) is found in several Icelandic works, most elaborately in the *Völsunga Saga*. But this dragon was once a man, a brother of Sigurd's foster father who became a dragon in order to guard a rich treasure and was mortally stabbed by Sigurd, then carried on a lengthy conversation with his slayer before dying. Compare this with the *Beowulf* poet's dragon and you have once again a sample of the poet's inventive powers. Dragons were of course familiar to Anglo-Saxons as large flying flame-throwing serpents who traditionally guarded treasures, but nowhere else in Germanic literature is there such a dragon as this.

OLD ENGLISH VERSE FORMS AND THIS TRANSLATION

Old English poetry has no stanzaic form and no rhyme (with the exception of a few later poems) except by accident. It consists of lines which run on to form sentences, each line composed of two half-lines, or verses, with a natural pause between them, so that the sentences may conclude at line-end or between half-lines. There is no set number of syllables per line—in *Beowulf* a normal line contains between eight and twelve. The half-lines are tied together by alliteration of consonants or vowels, any vowel alliterating with any other vowel through an emphatic pronunciation of stressed words that causes a sharp release of breath approximating a consonantal sound.

Each half-line has two strong stresses. Alliteration occurs only on stressed syllables. The first stress of the second half-line, called the "head-stave," cannot alliterate with the second stress of that half-line, but it must alliterate with one or both stressed syllables of the first half-line. Recitations of Old English poetry were accompanied in some way by a harplike instrument—indeed, it is called a *hearpe* in Old English—which may have been used to accentuate stresses, possibly to "fill in" for a missing stress in a defective half-line, but there is no way of knowing just how this was done.

Old English half-lines contain clearly defined stress patterns, bunching the two strong stresses at the beginning and then stepping down through secondary to weak, or bunching them both in the middle between weak stresses, or separating the two strong stresses with descending steps through secondary to weak, or approximating the Modern English iambic or trochaic measures. There are five of these patterns with a variation on one, some of them difficult to achieve in Modern English since secondary stress is not as clear or frequent today as it was a thousand years ago.

These half-lines, or verses, with their clearly defined rhythmic forms, are the primary building blocks of Old English poetry and derive from a strictly oral tradition of pagan Germanic poetry at a time when there were no manuscripts, when minstrels carried tales in their heads and recited long poems, partly from memory and partly through the use of an oral-formulaic system which permitted them to compose as they went along, drawing upon a large store of "prefabricated" half-lines or entire lines and mixing them with fresh inventions. Some entire lines are pale clichés, adding nothing to the poem, like "on that day of this life" (which occurs three times in *Beowulf*), but they give the minstrel time to think ahead. This is not peculiar to Germanic poetry—such lines are more frequent in the *Odyssey,* another poem derived from an ancient oral tradition, than in *Beowulf.*

Because of the primary importance of the half-lines, which must have been recited slowly and clearly with distinct stresses and a natural pause between them in most cases, they are separated in this translation by a space, as editors print the original. There is often a contrast between both the rhythm and the content of half-lines which also brings them together in a way difficult to describe, and sometimes they seem to float, repeating each other with variation and usually contrasting in rhythm, or acting as brief clauses with an absence of coordinates or subordinates that seems natural because of the pause between them in an oral presentation.

Since I am unaware of any translation of *Beowulf* that makes a serious attempt to imitate the original, I have tried in this translation to accomplish three things—to adhere strictly to the rules of alliteration, to imitate as closely as is practical the stress patterns of Old English half-lines, and to choose Modern English words and compounds that give at least some idea of the strength and radiance of the original while also reflecting the tone of the poem. A few restrictions upon the placement of unstressed syllables and requirements of quantity have been noted by modern scholars, and though these were certainly observed by the best poets, I have relaxed them at times to accommodate the stress patterns of Modern English and occasionally ignored other "rules" for the sake of a clear and forceful verse. I have often given up the secondary stress in one type of half-line (strong-secondary-weak-strong) because I had to choose between an awkwardly contrived verse and good words, and I usually chose the good words. Also, some "formulaic" half-lines are lacking a syllable when translated into Modern English (e.g., "Beowulf spoke" and "Ecgtheow's son") because I have preferred their simplicity to syllable counting.

Old English poetry cannot always be translated line by line, though this is sometimes possible if the words survive in Modern English. I have therefore not hesitated to translate words or half-lines from one line and place them two or three lines below or above in order to achieve the best effect. *Beowulf* is a poem, and what I have tried to produce here is another poem, closely reflective of the original. A line like *tholode thrythswyth   thegnsorge dreah* cannot be literally translated into prose or verse with anything like the effect of the original. It literally means "he suffered strength-strong   thane-sorrow he suffered," so that *thrythswyth,* a superb compound invented by the poet and composed of noun and adjective, is completely lost, and only the second compound may be salvaged. I have therefore translated "stooped in shadows stunned with thane-sorrow"—not literal but (I hope) decent poetry. I have also freely invented my own compounds, always attentive to both meaning and Old English poetic form, and have never misrepresented in any important way what is said or done in the poem.

I have respected the Old English spelling of names to retain the flavor of the original, but have stuck to one spelling throughout. I have silently compensated for manuscript corruption and destruction and have chosen what I consider to be the best interpretation of perplexing words, phrases, and sometimes entire sentences.

I have reluctantly inserted into the translation, at the beginning and in other places throughout, a few prose explanations of obscure passages that are important to the poem and were obviously clear enough to an Anglo-Saxon audience. I can think of no other device for solving this problem except the use of footnotes, which I dislike, or rewriting, expanding, and clarifying these passages, which would violate the poem and destroy their effect.

My debt to those who came before me is profound. The translation is based upon five modern editions of *Beowulf*—those of F. Klaeber, C. L. Wrenn, E. V. K. Dobbie, A. J. Wyatt as revised by R. W. Chambers, and the standard German edition by three successive editors referred to as the Heyne–Schücking–von Schaubert edition. My thinking over the years has been influenced by scores of essays, monographs, and books. Old English scholarship during the past century has been magnificent, and I would be lost without it.

One request: If readers will pause from time to time and read a few lines aloud, slowly and emphatically and with slight pauses between half-lines, they may find a faint echo of what a recitation probably sounded like, though the harp is forever silenced.

In "The Making of *Beowulf*," an inaugural lecture delivered at the University of Durham in 1961, G. V. Smithers said that "English literature begins with a masterpiece, which has no comparable Germanic antecedents in the same literary kind or form." *Beowulf* is indeed the first masterpiece in English, and it also had no followers, Germanic or otherwise, in the same literary kind or form. As I have said elsewhere, it seems to me that the poet is here presenting his personal elegy for the demise of an old and in many ways admirable tradition at the moment when it was giving in to and merging its best qualities with a new one. There is no other poem quite like it, and this translation has been done in honor of the nameless poet who created it, in an attempt to make his poem live again for the modern reader.

BEOWULF

A VERSE TRANSLATION

BEOWULF

Scyld Scefing, the first name mentioned in the poem, seems to come from the mists of legend. Later in the poem, a Danish king named Heremod, who died without an heir, is mentioned. Thus the mysterious arrival of Scyld, an unknown child drifting ashore in a boat, began a new dynasty. *Yrse,* the fourth child of Healfdene (whose name, not in the poem, is supplied from Norse tradition), was married to Onela, a Swedish king who plays a part in the final third of the poem.

The ominous words "Gables . . . waiting for hate-fire" refer to another Norse tradition, not developed in *Beowulf,* of a long-lasting feud between Danes and Heathobards. According to this tradition, Hrothgar marries his daughter to Ingeld, the new young king of the Heathobards, but this merely postpones hostilities, and the Heathobards attack, burning Heorot, though they are finally vanquished. Upon Hrothgar's death, his nephew Hrothulf takes the throne and kills Hrethric, Hrothgar's elder son. Hrothgar's younger son Hrothmund and his other nephew Heoroweard are also in line for the throne. These four people are merely referred to in the poem with portentous overtones.

The descent of Grendel and other monsters from Cain after the

1

biblical flood is explained in the early Middle Ages by the corrup-
tion of Noah's son Ham, whose offspring continued the breed of
monsters begun with Cain.

I

Yes! We have heard   of years long vanished
how Spear-Danes struck   sang victory-songs
raised from a wasteland   walls of glory.
Then Scyld Scefing   startled his neighbors
measured meadhalls   made them his own
since down by the sea-swirl   sent from nowhere
the Danes found him   floating with gifts
a strange king-child.   Scyld grew tall then
roamed the waterways   rode through the land
till every strongman   each warleader
sailed the whalepaths   sought him with gold
there knelt to him.   That was a king!
Time brought to him   birth for his people
a gift to the Danes   who had grieved throne-sorrows
cold and kingless—the Keeper of men
softened their longing   with Scyld's man-child
sunlight in their hearts.   To this son the Wielder
Life-Lord of men   loaned strength-wisdom
banishing the ache   of a barren meadhall.
Beaw was nimble   his name went traveling
sung wide and far   in the world's kingdom.
So should a prince   show his heartstrength
by his father's side   share gold-treasures
forge friend-warriors   to fight against darkness
in his last winters.   With love and action
shall a man prevail   in memory and song.
At the hour shaped for him   Scyld took his leave
a kingly departure   to the King's embrace.

10

20

2

They bore their savior   back to the sea
his bones unburned   as he bade them do
child of the mist   who chased their mourning
loved and led them   through the long winters.
Ready at seashore   stood a ring-prowed ship
icy and eager   armed for a king.
They braced him then   once bright with laughter
shaper of hall-songs   on the ship's middle-board
hard by the mast.   From hills and valleys
rings and bracelets   were borne to the shore.
No words have sung   of a wealthier grave-ship
bright with war-weapons   ballasted with gold
swords and ring-mail   rich for drifting
through the foaming tide   far from that land.
Their lord was laden   for long sailpaths
with love and sorrow   splendid with gifts
for those who had ferried him   far through the mist
once sent them a sailor   strange treasure-child.
At last they hung   high upon the mast
a golden banner   then gave him to the sea
to the mounding waves.   Their mindgrief was great
mood was mourning.   Men cannot know
cannot truthfully say—singers of tales
sailors or gleemen—who gathered him in.
Then Beaw held them   banished war-ravens
sailed through the summers   strengthening peace
like his father before him   known far abroad
a king to contend with.   Time brought a son
high-minded Healfdene   who held in his turn
through long glory-years   the life-line of Scyld.
Then four strong ones   came forth from his queen
woke to the world   warmed the gift-hall—
Heorogar and Hrothgar   Halga the good
Yrse the fair one   Onela's hall-queen

3

that battle-wise Swede's   bed-companion.
Hrothgar was beckoned   born for a kingdom
shaped as a lord   loved by his hall-thanes
who bore him high   as boys became men
and men grew mighty.   His mind told him
to raise a throne-house   rarest in Denmark
mightiest meadhall   in measure and strength
that the oldest among them   ever had beheld
to give freely   what God had provided
share his wealth there   shape borderlands
love and lead them   in light against darkness.
Then, as I heard,   help came crowding
from hills and glens   hewers of timber
trimmers and weavers.   It towered at last
highest of them all—Heorot he named it
who with words wielded   the world of the Danes.
Hrothgar was king   kept his promise
gave from his gift-throne   goldgifts and peace.
Gables were crossed   capped with horn-beams,
waiting for hate-fire   high anger-flames.
It was yet too soon   for swordswings to clash
not yet the day   for dark throne-battle
a blood-minded son   and his bride's father.
Then an alien creature   cold wanderer
could no longer endure   from his dark exile
bright bench-laughter   borne to the rafters
each night in that hall.   The harp sounded
the poet's clear song.   He sang what he knew
of man's creation   the Measurer's work:
"He shaped the earth   opened the heavens
rounded the land   locked it in water
then set skyward   the sun and the moon
lights to brighten   the broad earthyard
beckoned the ground   to bear gardens

of limbs and leaves—life He created
of every kind   that quickens the earth."
They lived brightly   on the benches of Heorot
100 caught up in laughter   till a creature brought them
fear in the night   an infernal hall-guest.
Grendel circled   sounds of the harp
prowled the marshes   moors and ice-streams
forests and fens.   He found his home
with misshapen monsters   in misery and greed.
The Shaper banished him   unshriven away
with the kin of Cain   killer of his blood.
The Measurer fashioned   a fitting revenge
for the death of Abel   drove his slayer
110 far from mankind   and far from His grace.
Cain sired evil   cunning man-killers
banished from heartlove   born in hatred
giants and fiends   jealous man-eaters
long without penance.   God paid them for that.
Then Grendel prowled,   palled in darkness,
the sleep-warm hall   to see how the Ring-Danes
after beer and feasting   bedded down for rest.
He found inside   slumbering warriors
unready for murder.   Bereft of remorse
120 from love exiled   lost and graceless
he growled with envy   glared above them
towering with rage.   From their rest he snared
thirty hall-thanes   loped howling away
gloating with corpses   galloping the moors
back to his cavern   for a cold banquet.
At dawning of day   when darkness lifted
Grendel's ravage   rose with the sun.
The waking Danes   wailed to the heavens
a great mourning-song.   Their mighty ruler
130 lord of a death-hall   leaned on his grief

5

stooped in shadows   stunned with thane-sorrow
bent to the tracks   of his baneful houseguest
no signs of mercy.   His mind was too dark
nightfall in his heart.   There was no need to wait
when the sun swung low   for he slaughtered again
murdered and feasted   fled through nightmist
damned to darkness   doomed with a curse.
It was easy to find   those who elsewhere slept
sought distant rest   reached for night-cover
140 found beds with others   when the bad news came
the lifeless messages   left by that caller
murderous hall-thane.   Men still walking
kept from the shadows   no shame in their hearts.
Now a lone rage-ruler   reigned through the night
one against them all   till empty and still
stood the long meadhall.   Too long it stood
twelve cold winters   wound in despair—
the lord of the Danes   dreamed of his lost ones
waited for a sign.   Then it widely was known
150 in dark Denmark   that death lived with them
when weeping heartsongs   wailed of Grendel
Hrothgar's hall-monster   hell's banquet-guest—
lashed by hunger   he longed for nightfall
with no pause or pity,   poison in his heart.
No plans for payment   passed through that mind
money or goldgifts   remorse for slaughter—
no somber mourners   sued for revenge
death-settlement   from that demon's hands.
He raged at them all   envious hell-fiend
160 in dark death-shadow   doomed young and old
trapped and snared them   trailed in nightshade
cloud-misted moors—no man can follow
where God's enemies   glide through the fog.
Dawn brought to them   blood-signs of his rage—

6

outcast from grace   Grendel went prowling
the empty hall-benches.   Heorot received him
in cold darkness   damned to his rule.
Yet he never could greet   the peaceful gift-throne
love and bounty   life-joy and gold
170 for the old betrayal   outlawed him there.
It was long despair   for the lord of the Danes
a breaking of mind.   Many a counselor
gathered to whisper   groped for messages
ways to escape   those woeful night-visits.
Some made promises   prayed to idols
swore to honor them   asked them for help
safety from murder.   Such was their custom
the hope of heathens   hell-thoughts in their minds.
They ignored the Measurer   Maker of heaven
180 Shaper of glory   stuck to their gods
unable to praise   or pray to the Father
wish for his guidance.   Woe unto those
with ill in their hearts   hopeless and doomed
forcing their souls   to the fire's welcome
praying to names   that will never help them
praise without hope.   Happier are they
who seek after deathday   the Deemer of men
free their soul-bonds   to the Father's embrace.
With sinking heart   the son of Healfdene
190 endlessly waited   wept for an answer
with no hope for relief.   Too long and merciless
slaughter and greed   seemed to his people
narrow and endless   nightbale and tears.

In the home of the Geats   Hygelac's thane
gathered the stories   of Grendel's torment
a good man and strong   strongest of all
in that broad kingdom   born for deliverance

7

shaped for that hour.   He ordered a boat
lithe wave-cutter   loudly proclaimed
200 he would seek the Battle-Danes   sail the waveswells
hail their king there   kindle their hearts.
Though they loved him   life-seasoned elders
answered his courage   urged him onwards
gazed at the weather   gave heart-blessings.
With care this champion   chose his spearmen
culled from the Geats   their keenest fighters
good men and faithful.   Fifteen in all
they sought their seacraft   strode to the cliffs
followed their chief   to the fallow waves.
210 Fast by the headland   their hard-keeled boat
waited for westering.   Winding in swirls
the sea met the sand.   They stored their weapons
bright shields gleaming   spears and helmets
strong war-weapons.   Shoved through the breakers
the stout-bound wood   slid from the land.
They flew on the water   fast by the wind blown
sail flecked with foam   swam with birdwing
through day and darkness.   Dawn grayed the sky
and the hour grew near   when over the wave-tops
220 the coiled bowsprit   brought them a sign.
A rising of land   reached towards the sun
shining seacliffs   steep rock-pillars
bound with shoresand.   The sail grew limp
shallows lapped at them.   Leaping to the sand
the Weather-Geats waded   walked their ship up
lashed it to land.   Linked steel-corselets
clinked and glistened.   They gave thanks then
to the God of them all   for guiding them safely.
Watching above them   the warden of the shores
230 glimpsed from the cliff-top   a glinting of armor
as they bore from their boat   bright shields and spears

8

rich with war-weapons.   He wrenched his thoughts
groped within his mind   who these men might be.
He roused his horse then   rode to the seashore—
Hrothgar's cliff-guardian   heaved up his spear
shook it to the sky   and spoke this question:
"Who might you be   in your burnished mailcoats
shining with weapons?   Who steered this warboat
deep-running keel   across the waveswells

240   here against this shore?   I assure you now
I've held this guard-post   hard against sailors
watched over Denmark   down through the years
that no hateful shipband   might harbor unfought.
Never have boatmen   beached more openly
shield-bearing thanes   unsure of your welcome
hoisting no signal   to hail peace-tokens
friendship to the Danes.   I doubt that I've challenged
a loftier shieldman   than your leader there
hale in his war-gear—no hall-lounger that

250   worthied with weapons—may his wit not belie
so handsome a swordman.   I will hear quickly
first where you came from   before you move on
you possible pirates   pushing further
into Danish land.   Now let me advise you
horseless sailors   hear my counsel
my heartfelt words: Haste will be best
in letting me know   the land you came from."
The ablest among them   answered him clearly
lifted up his spear   unlocked his wordhoard:

260   "We are mindful of manners   men of the Geats
Lord Hygelac's   hearth-companions.
My father wandered   far through this world
earned his way there   Ecgtheow by name
survived many winters   wartime and peace
till age wearied him.   He won many battles

9

named by Northmen   in nations abroad.
Now we have come here   with kind intentions
to seek out your lord   son of Healfdene
victor of men.   Advise us well!
270 We bear to your lord   leader of the Danes
a helpful message—but we hold no secrets
now that we're here.   You know if it's true
stories told to us   sorrowful tales
evil in Denmark   some demon or giant
a devilish creature   who in darkness of night
roams the moorpaths   murder in his heart
hell's messenger.   To Hrothgar I offer
words to consider   serious counsel
how this wise ruler   may win over deathdays
280 if an end to sorrows   ever will come forth
a taming of torment   time for revenge
healing of heartbreak   in this helpless land.
Unless this happens   as long as he rules
darkness and bloodgrief   will doom his people
banished forever   from that best of halls."
The coastguard replied   proud horse-soldier
no fear in his words: "One way or another
a sharp warden   can weigh carefully
words and intentions   if he's worthy in thought.
290 I've heard in your speech   heartstrong fealty
to the lord of the Danes.   I'll lead you now
with your spears and helmets   to the hall above—
I'll tell my companions   to tend to your ship
guard carefully   against all comers
this newly tarred vessel   nestled in sand
to hold it in trust   till the time comes round
when homeward it bears   the best among you
brings back alive   beloved warriors

on this ring-prowed ship   riding foamwaves
300   back to the Weather-Geats   wondering for news."
They marched forward then   mounted the headland
left their keel-ship   lashed to beach-anchor
roped to the sand.   Around their mask-helmets
golden boar-heads   beamed to the sun
flashed a war-gleam   on fire-hardened steel
signaled their weapons.   They walked strong-stepping
crested the sea-wall   till they saw the glinting
of that timber-strong hall   trimmed bright with gold
tall horn-gables   towering in the sun
310   high to the heavens   Hrothgar's gift-house—
its light shone forth   over land and sea.
The coastguard paused   pulled his horse round
hefted his spear   towards the hall beyond
stopped by the road   ready for their footsteps
paused for a moment   with these parting words:
"Fare you well now—may the Father almighty
hold you from harm   help from this moment
teach you the way.   I turn to the sea
back to the beaches   bastions of Denmark."
320   The stone-cobbled road   ran on before them
as they marched together.   Their mailcoats glistened
laced by smith-hands—linked steel-jackets
clinked an armor-song   as they came to the hall
strode in their war-gear   straight to the door.
They settled broadshields   bright against the wall
rounded and hardened   by ringing forge-hammers.
They bent to the benches   breast-coats in rows
life-guarding corselets.   They leaned ash-spears
ranked by the door   reaching above them
330   gray-tipped treelimbs.   Geats rested there
wealthy in weapons.   A warrior came forth

eager for news-words   asked who they were:
"From where have you brought   those broad-rimmed
    shields
gray-gleaming mailcoats   good mask-helmets
such a heap of armor?   I am Hrothgar's
counselor and friend.   How far have you traveled
crossed the wave-rolls   to come to this door?
My wits tell me   you are welcome callers
in full friendship   no fugitives with you."

340   The chief of the Geats   gave him an answer
tall and helmeted   taught him with words
the meaning of his men: "We are mighty Hygelac's
board-companions—Beowulf is my name.
I have come to greet   your great people-king
to tell your Dane-lord   tidings of hope
explain to your king   if he plans to receive us
why we sailed westward   to this splendid meadhall."
Wulfgar replied   watchful Northman
son of the Wendels   wearing their strength

350   no hurry in his mind: "I will hail my chief
mournful of murder   mix words with him
greet the gift-throne   give him your name
since you sailed this far   to share his heartgrief.
I will step to the high-seat   stand before him
bear his answer   back to you here."
He entered the hall   where Hrothgar sorrowed,
gray in his mindthoughts   grief cloaking him,
strode to the gift-throne   stepped before him
skilled in the customs   of kings of the North.

360   Wulfgar spoke then   words mixed with light:
"Here we have strangers   hailing from far
sailing the gulfstreams   from Geatish country.
The greatest among them   as I gauge the man
is known as Beowulf.   They bring hope-tidings

wish to share words   wait peacefully
to greet you, my lord.   Do not leave them there
but give them welcome   gladman Hrothgar!
Their weapons shine   steel boar-helmets
gleaming with gold.   Their Geatish king
370   is a prosperous man   a mighty ruler."
Hrothgar answered   helm of the Danes:
"I knew their chieftain   a child long ago.
His father was Ecgtheow   who found his wife
in the hall of the Geats   where Hrethel gave him
his only daughter.   This day his son
has come to find me   a friend of his youth.
Sailors have told me,   sea-messengers
ferrying gifts   from Götland to Denmark
with thankful tokens,   that this tall grappler
380   can grind as strongly   in the grip of his hand
as thirty war-thanes.   I think that the Measurer
Maker of us all   has urged him here,
sent to the Danes,   I dare to imagine,
relief from Grendel.   For this great mercy
I promise him now   priceless heirlooms.
Make haste, my friend,   fetch them in here
all of them together   to greet all of us,
tell them clearly   that they come as lamplight
to darkness in Heorot."   To the door he turned
390   Wulfgar the Wendel   wove them a speech:
"My lord has told me   my beloved hearth-king
chief of the East-Danes   that he honors your kin.
You have come in time,   the tide has brought you
like welling waves   welcome to his heart.
Come forth with me   in your corselets of steel
your hard mask-helmets   where Hrothgar awaits you.
Leave your shield-boards   your spears by the benches
until you have traded   talk with my lord."

13

Some remained there   stayed by their weapons
400 held them from harm.   Their hero rose then,
around him his thanes   ready for orders.
They walked together   Wulfgar before them
under Heorot's roof   helmets gleaming
stood at the hearth   hard by the gift-throne.
Beowulf spoke then,   burnished mailcoat
work of wonder-smiths   winking in firelight:
"Hail to you, Hrothgar!   I am Hygelac's thane
nephew-kin and friend.   I have known much peril
grim death-dangers.   Grendel's ravages
410 came to my ears   in my own homeland.
Sailors have said   that this strong meadhall
with high gold-gables   this Hall of the Hart
stands empty and idle   when evening-light fades
when the dark sky lowers   and light thins to gray.
My people have urged me,   elders and youth
best of Weather-Geats   brothers of my heart,
to cross the gulfway   come straight to you
offer you my strength   stand by your side.
They saw for themselves   as I surfaced from ambush
420 broke through the waves   to the winds of sunrise
how I crushed water-sprites   cracked their blood-teeth
shoved them deathwards   down by the sea-floor
fought them by night   in narrow-dark waters
on the sandy ground.   Grendel is next—
I will settle alone   this sorrowful feud
this baleful business.   I beg of you now
lord of the Ring-Danes   royal man-leader
a small favor-gift   from sovereign to friend—
do not refuse me   now that I'm here
430 come from afar   to cancel your problem—
I and my men   no more than this war-band

14

will cleanse your Heorot   close out this evil.
I also have heard   that this hellish monster
with careless strength   carries no weapons.
I will therefore swear   in honor of Hygelac—
to keep my protector   proud in his heart—
I'll bear no swordblade   no shield to that fight
no boar-head helmet—with my handgrip only
I will fight this fiend   find his life-core
440   man against monster.   Tomorrow you will find
at rising of light   the Ruler's judgment.
If this demon wins   no doubt he will banquet
on bodies of Geats   gorge with all of us
swill and swallow   snatch our lives away
munch on our bones.   Do not mourn for me
or search for my head   in shadows of defeat
if he cracks my bones   bends me deathwards
hauls me away   hoping to taste me
slash me to morsels   with murder in his heart
450   staining the moors.   Do not sorrow for long
for my lifeless body   lost and devoured.
But send to Hygelac   if struggle takes me
this best of battle-shrouds   breast-protector
greatest of corselets   good Hrethel's gift
Weland's hand-smithing.   Wyrd is determined!"
Hrothgar answered   helm of the Danes:
"Beowulf my friend   you have brought from home
a gesture of honor   joining with us now.
Your father once caused   the cruelest of feuds—
460   his hands emptied   Heatholaf's lifeblood
a man of the Wylfingas.   The Weather-Geats then
dared not hold him   for the harm he caused.
From there he sought   the South-Danes' country—
over angry waves   the winds delivered him.

15

I first ruled then   the realm of my people
held in my youth   a young kingdom
homeland of the Danes—Heorogar was dead
my older brother   born of Healfdene
borne to the grave—he was better than me!
470 I managed that feud   fixed it with payment
sent to the Wylfingas   sailors with gifts
saved your good father   with fine peace-tokens.
It wounds me to say   weary with mourning
aching with grief   how Grendel comes calling
each twilight in Heorot   tortures us all
with nightblack murders.   My men are fewer
some carried away—wyrd has swept them
into Grendel's grasp.   God could easily
stem this heart-sickness   sweep it away.
480 Often my hall-thanes   hearts strong with beer
bold in their ale-cups   boasted in firelight
that they would linger   lie here in waiting
for Grendel's ravaging   ready with swordswings.
Then was this meadhall   at morning's raven-call
dark with their doom   as the day shoved forth,
benches and bolsters   black with battle-gore
hall-rafters red-stained.   Heorot grew cold then
stronghearted warriors   were snatched into night.
But sit now to banquet   bear us good news
490 tell us good tidings   in time as you wish."
Benches were bared   the beer-hall made roomy
Geats were gathered   together with all.
There the stern-hearted   settled by the fire
welcome and ready.   The warden of ale-cups
brought to their hands   the bright hall-drink
tended to their needs.   At times the minstrel
touched his harpstrings.   They were happy together
a great band of them   Geats with the Danes.

UNFERTH (meaning "discord" or "nonsense") is a complex character who is twice called a *thyle* ("orator" or "jester") and sits at Hrothgar's feet, a position of counselors or jesters or poets. Here he is the traditional "court challenger," enabling Beowulf to establish his credentials as a monster killer and giving him license to insult both Unferth and the Danes with impunity. Beowulf calls him a fratricide who will suffer either "in hell" or "in the hall," depending on how the manuscript is interpreted, and it is later said that he was "not honorable towards his kin in swordplay." This may mean that he found himself serving one lord and his brothers another, or he may have refused to support his brothers in battle. In any case, Unferth is well tolerated by the Danes and lends his respected sword to a grateful Beowulf.

Before and after the killing of Grendel, Hrothgar leaves Heorot to sleep in his "bower," an outbuilding within the palisade compound characteristic of many Anglo-Saxon "burgs."

Then up spoke Unferth   Ecglaf's swordson
500   held to his station   at Hrothgar's feet
unbound battle-runes.   Beowulf's errand
boasting of sea-strength   burned in his heart—
never would he grant   greater adventures
on land or sea   to sailors or hall-thanes
than he had survived,   hale sword-champion:
"Are you that Beowulf   who with Breca swam
on the broad sea-swell   struggling together
proud wave-wrestlers   wagering your lives
with reckless boasting   risking for praise
510   deep water-death?   Not one counselor
friend or enemy   could force you to cancel
that sorrowful swim—shipless wanderers
rowing with your hands   reaching for salt-swells
measuring the sea-road   with stroking arms
embracing the ocean   broad water-fields
wintry with waves.   You worked at your folly
for seven nightfalls—he outswam you there

stronger than you.   The sea at dawning
heaved him ashore   on Heatho-Raemas' ground.
520 He found his way then   fared to his home
beloved country   land of the Brondingas
proud timber-hall   where his people waited.
That son of Beanstan   beat you at swimming
bettered your boasting   brave sea-warrior.
Now I expect,   proud though you swagger,
brave at battle-rush   bragging as you go,
a grimmer contest   with Grendel here
if you dare sleep now   in this darkened hall."
Beowulf answered   Ecgtheow's son:
530 "Unferth my friend   you find much to say
eased with beer-cups   all about Breca
his seafaring ways.   I say to you now
I was greater in swim-strength   gliding through the waves
swifter at arm-strokes   than my swim companion.
We boasted together—boys eagering
young in judgment   yearning for renown
game for water-wolves—that we would gamble
lives against the sea   loud ocean winds.
With naked swords   we slashed through the waves
540 ready with warblades   for wandering whales
dark sea-monsters.   No swifter than me
could Breca swim there—I stayed beside him
unwilling to leave him   alone against all.
Through five nightfalls   we floated and swam
on the ice-hard waves   till an angry sea-flood
broke out above us—blackening sky
and freezing northwinds   forced us apart
towering salt-swells   struck between us.
Strange sea-creatures   surfaced around me—
550 the mailcoat I wore   woven with gold
hard and hand-locked   held me from death

18

laced by wonder-smiths   linked shroud-cover.
To the deep sea-floor   something pulled me
hard gripfingers   hauled me to sand
with grappling-tight claws—it was granted to me
to reach this devil   rush him to sleep
with sharp sword-point—swift blade-slashing
strong in my hand   haled him deathwards.
Then more came at me   many a water-sprite
560   seagoing demons—I served them all
with quick sword-thrusts   sent them to hell.
They missed their supper   sea-bottom banquet
squatting on the sand   serving their hunger
with my tasty corpse   cold ocean-feast.
By the sea-dawn's light   lapped with salt-foam
rolled by the waves   they rested on the beach
sleepened by swordswings—the sailpath was cleared
sun-bright waterways   washed of their blood.
Light from the East   lifted the storm-clouds
570   God's bright beacon   burnished the sea—
looming headlands   leaned high above
wind-scoured cliffwalls.   Wyrd often spares
an undoomed man   when his mind-strength prevails.
With sword's edges   I sent into death
nine sea-monsters.   Never have I heard
of a harder struggle   under heaven's archway
a riskier night   in narrow ocean-streams.
From dark water-death   waves bore me up
weary of swimming—the sea lifted me
580   led me to shore   in the land of Finns.
I have never heard tell   tales of yourself
terrible swordplay   swimming through the night
with gnashing sea-demons.   Never has Breca
fought through darkness   in deep waterways—
and you were never   known for such deeds

19

nothing to brag of   renowned as you are
for killing your brothers   bringing them down,
your own blood-kin.   You'll answer for that
wandering in hell   though your wit be strong.
590 I'll say one thing   son of Ecglaf—
never would Grendel   grieve all of you
mangle your hearts   with murder in Heorot
torture your lord   in this tame meadhall
if your courage held strong   as you claim it does.
Grendel has learned   through long winters—
no need to bother   with brave Shield-Danes
no interruptions   of his nightly visits.
He takes what he needs   no one stopping him
finds no contest   with cowering Danes
600 snares and slashes   safe in Heorot
owning you all.   But I'll show him
sooner than he knows   a new kind of battle
with men of the Geats.   On the morning after
when southern sunlight   shines on this hall
we will lift our meadcups   to merciful peace
bright bench-laughter   banishing your grief."
Mind-weary Hrothgar   murder-gray king
heard in those words   hard promises
news of deliverance   from long heartbreak
610 found in Beowulf   fair morning-thoughts.
Laughter and song   leapt to the rafters
warm welcome-words.   Then Wealhtheow came forth
folk-queen of the Danes   daughter of Helmingas
Hrothgar's bedmate.   She hailed all of them
spoke her peace-words   stepped to the gift-throne
fetched to her king   the first ale-cup
warmed his mind-chill   wished darkness away
from the tall high-seat—he took from her hands
the gleaming cupful   gave her his thanks.

20

620 Through the high meadhall   went Hrothgar's queen
offering hall-joy   to old and to young
with rich treasure-cups   till time brought her
where Beowulf sat.   She bore him a cup
with gold-gleaming hands   held it before him
graciously greeted   the Geats' warleader
gave thanks to God   for granting her will
faith in mercy   a man to believe in
hope from abroad.   He held the meadcup
high in his hands   hailed the queen there
630 brought to Wealhtheow   battle-hearty words.
Beowulf spoke   son of Ecgtheow:
"I swore to myself   when I sailed from home
mounted my ship   with my men around me
that I alone   would ease your heartgrief
settle this feud here   or fall deathwards
in Grendel's grasp.   I'll give you his lifeblood
deliver his fiend-soul   or finish my days
here in Heorot   high treasure-hall."
His words were welcome   to Wealhtheow's heart
640 that bountiful boast—then back with her lord
that proud folk-queen   found her station.
Cheers from the benches   chased night-shadows
strong warrior-songs   soared through the hall
rose to the rafters   till ready for sleep
Healfdene's son   heavy with thane-grief
yearned for evening-rest.   Years had taught him
that Grendel roamed   raging with envy
Heorot on his mind   from the moment that sunrise
flushed towards the sky   till final nightshades
650 dark with shadow-shapes   slid across the meadows
claiming the night-sky.   Hall-feasters rose.
Their weary war-king   wished for Beowulf
luck in the night   left him the gift-throne

21

that great meadhall   gave him farewell:
"Never have I offered   to any other man,
from the first moment   I found shield-strength,
this hall of the Danes   house of our nation.
Have now and hold   these havoc-stained walls
remember your strength   stand against darkness
660 with luck and courage.   You will lack for nothing
if you risk this nightfall   and rise with the sun."
He left the hall then   Healfdene's son
lord of the Shield-Danes   beloved treasure-king
went to his bedrest   Wealhtheow beside him
sought comfort with his queen.   The King of glory
granted for that night   a guard against helldeath
a strong hall-warden   holding in darkness
a keen house-watch   for the king of Heorot.
The Geats' champion   gathered his courage
670 matched against evil   the Measurer's strength.
He stripped off his armor   steel-meshed mailcoat
gilded mask-helmet   gold-handled sword
set them aside   to serve him elsewhere
rich war-weapons   wonder-smiths' handwork.
He kindled their courage   with keen boastwords
as they bent to bedrest   in that best of halls:
"No meaner am I   in mortal combat
grim hand-wrestling   than Grendel himself.
I will not send him   to sleep with my blade
680 carve out his life   though I could easily.
He has learned nothing   of linden-shields and swords
fighting with armor   fearless though he be
in dark thane-murder—on this dangerous night
we'll have no swordplay   if he seeks me here
no clear weapon-fight—then the wise Deemer
will decide between us   the Shaper of us all
will measure us both   bring judgment here."

22

He bent to his bolster   Beowulf the Geat
put his head to rest—around him battle-friends
690   stouthearted sailors   settled down to sleep.
Not one believed   they would leave Heorot
take ship once more   seek out their homeland
the known meadows   of their native country.
Too many stories   of that tall wine-hall
emptied of Danes   by dark night-slaughter
had found their ears.   But the Father of men
wove them battle-speed—Weather-Geats prevailed
reprieved from hate-death   haled to victory
by the strength of one   saved from farewell
700   by a tight handgrip.   It truly is known
that God manages   men of this earth.

He slipped through the darkness   under deep nightpall
sliding through shadows.   Shield-warriors rested
slumbering guardians   of that gabled hall—
all except one.   That wandering spirit
could never drag them   to cold death-shadow
if the world's Measurer   wished to stop him.
(A waking warrior   watched among them
anger mounting   aching for revenge.)
710   He moved through the mist   past moors and ice-streams
Grendel gliding   God's wrath on him
simmering to snare   some sleeping hall-thanes
trap some visitors   in that tall gift-house.
He moved under cloudbanks   crossed the meadowlands
till the wine-hall towered   tall gold-gables
rising in night-sky.   Not for the first time
he came to Heorot   Hrothgar's gift-hall—
never had he come   craving a blood-feast
with worse slaughter-luck   waiting there inside.
720   He came to the hall   hungry for man-flesh

23

exiled from joy.   The ironbound door
smith-hammered hinges   sprang at his touch—
raging then for gore   he gripped in his hand-vice
the ruined bolt-work   wrenched it away
leapt into the hall   loomed with blood-rage
aching with life-lust—from his eyes shone forth
a fearful glowering   fire-coals smoldering.
Near him he spied   sleeping together
close war-brothers   waiting peacefully
730   prime for plucking.   He exploded with fury
growled with greed-hunger   glared all around him
burning to separate   bodies from life-breath
drain blood-vessels   before breaking of day.
His luck left him   on that last slaughter-night—
no more after sunrise   would he murder and run.
Wakeful and watching   wonder in his mind
Hygelac's nephew   held to his bedrest
anxious to measure   that monster's strength.
Nor did that thief   think about waiting
740   but searched with fire-eyes   snared a doomed one
in terminal rest   tore frantically
crunched bonelockings   crammed blood-morsels
gulped him with glee.   Gloating with his luck
he finished the first one   his feet and his hands
swallowed all of him.   He stepped closer
groped with claw-hands   grabbed the next one—
the watchful Geat   grabbed back at him
gripped with his fingers   that great demon-hand
tightened his grasp   tugged steadily.
750   Soon that fen-stalker   found himself caught
grasped and twisted   by a greater handgrip
than any he had known   in the earth's regions
iron finger-clamps—into his mind
fear came nudging—nowhere could he move.

His thoughts yearned away   he wished for his mere-den
devils' company—doubt pulled at him
a new sensation   slid into his mind.
Then Hygelac's thane   held to his boasting
mindful of his speech   stood quickly then
760 tightened his fist—fingers crackled
Grendel pulled back   Beowulf followed.
That dark wanderer   wished for more room
to be on his way   back to the moor-hills
flee to the fens.   He felt his knuckles
crushed in that grip.   A grim visitor
that fate-marked fiend   found in Heorot.
The hall thundered—to hovering Danes
safe hut-dwellers   sounds of that battle
clattered and roared.   They raged together
770 warrior and guest—the walls rumbled.
With great wonder   the wine-hall survived
twin horn-gables   trembling with combat
towering high above—it held steadily
inside and out   with iron log-bonds
forged by smith-hammers.   The floor shuddered
strong mead-benches   sailed to the walls
gold-trimmed banquet-seats   bounced and clattered.
Hrothgar's wisemen   hallowed counselors
had never believed   that a living creature
780 might break Heorot   bring down the walls—
only fire's embrace   flames' greediness
could swallow that hall.   Storm-sounds of death
rocked the horn-gables   hammered the roof—
shivering Danefolk   shook with hell-fear
heard through the walls   a wailing sorrow.
God's demon-foe   ground his blood-teeth
howled to be gone   home to the ice-streams
far from that hall.   Hygelac's thane

strongest mortal   mightiest of hand
790   locked that hell-fiend   hard within his grasp.
He found no reason   to free that monster
spare him to flee   far across the moors
nor did he consider   that sinful life
useful to anyone.   Anxious for their leader
men of the Geats   grabbed treasure-swords
lifted them high   to help their champion
fight for his life   with file-hardened edges.
They were not prepared   for this new hand-battling
those hard-swinging swordmen   hewing with steel-bites
800   slashing about them   with shield-breaking cuts
seeking that fiend-soul—they fought without knowing
that the choicest of blades   champions' war-weapons
were helpless to harm   that hell's messenger.
He had cast his spell   on keenest thane-weapons
finest treasure-swords   though his time was short—
that final night-visit   finished his hall-raids
destiny struck   his damned hell-soul
banished it forever   past boundaries of grace.
Then that giant ravager   rejected by God
810   marked with murder   measured by his sins
finally conceived   in his fiend's mindthoughts
that his loathsome body   would bear no more.
Hygelac's thane   held fast to him
tightened his grip—Grendel yearned away
his arm stretched thin   thronging with pain—
a great death-wound   gaped in his shoulder
sinew-bonds weakened   snapped viciously
bonelockings burst.   To Beowulf there
victory was granted.   Grendel fled then
820   sickened with death   slouched under fen-slopes
to his joyless home   no hope for his life—
he knew at last   the number of his days.

To the Danes' misery   a dawning of mercy
rose from that battle   bright deliverance.
Heorot was cleansed   healed of thane-sorrow
aching morning-grief   emptied of murder
by that tall visitor—victory was bright
joy to his heart.   He held to his promise,
evening boastwords,   banished from that hall
830   dark sorrow-songs   consoled the Danes
for long torture-years   terror in the night
an empty meadhall   from evening till dawn.
He hailed the sunrise   hoisted a signal
a clear token-sign   that terror was dead
nailed Grendel's arm   that great handgrip
near the high gable-point   of Heorot's roof.
By morning's light   many a warrior
gathered watchfully   by the gift-hall's door.
Chieftains and followers   from far and from near
840   gazed at that wonder   grisly monster-arm
hand and knife-claws   high death-trophy.
Grendel's life-loss   gladdened the Danes
who followed his footprints   where he fled to his death
left his sorrow-tracks   staining the moors
went back to the mere   bleak monster-home
teeming with nicors   tomb of the damned.
The water-top trembled   welling with blood
roiled restlessly   with red venom-waves
hot demon-gore   heaved from the depths—
850   Grendel was deathwards   doomed man-killer
laid down his life   in that loathsome fen-pond—
hell received him   and his heathen soul.
They turned away   wonder in their hearts—
old counselors   carried by horses
many a young one   mounted beside them
turned back from the mere.   Beowulf's renown

filled their mindthoughts—many a Spear-Dane
mindful of that night   remembering hell-years
swore that no man   under mighty heaven
860   from south or north   on sea or on land
was greater in battle   than Beowulf the Geat.
Nor did they blame   their bountiful lord
gladman Hrothgar   good man and king.

HROTHGAR'S MINSTREL now improvises a song of Beowulf, then moves on
to the dragon slayer Sigemund (an early legendary Danish hero) and his
nephew Fitela, who shared his adventures after the dragon slaying, thus
praising the victory over Grendel and anticipating Beowulf's final battle.
This is the earliest literary account of the famous Völsung family (Waels-
ing in *Beowulf*), later versions of which portray Sigemund's son Sigurd
(later Siegfried) as the dragon slayer.

At times the riders   ready for contest
let their war-steeds   leap to the race
where broad meadowlands   bright grass-tables
widened the trail.   At times the minstrel
heavy with memory   mindful of the past,
ancient war-sagas   old monster-tales,
870   wove his verse-songs—one word found another
skillfully bound.   He sang at first
of Beowulf's valor   victory in Heorot
death of a monster   and his dark water-home
a champion's tale.   He told what he knew
stories he had heard   of Sigemund the Dane
marvelous moments   of mighty sword-feats
Waelsing's adventures   wide traveling
secret wanderings   seldom disclosed
except to Fitela   faithful companion
880   when he fell to telling   tales of his youth
to his only shield-friend   always by his side—

uncle and nephew   in narrow adventures
seeking forest-fiends   strange wood-giants
ending them with swords.   After his deathday
Sigemund's renown   was sung in battle-songs
tales of dragon-breath   days of sword-slaughter
glorious rewards.   Under gray barrow-stone
he gambled his life   gathered his courage
fought against his fate   nor was Fitela with him.
It chanced that his sword-point   struck through the flesh
pierced that serpent   struck in the barrow-wall—
that marvelous dragon   died of murder.
Sigemund survived   unsinged by that breath
earned a treasure-mound   for his own delight
a loan from destiny.   He loaded a boat
bore to its bosom   the bright slaughter-prize
that serpent's goldnest—the steaming dragon
monstrously hot   melted to the ground.
The wandering Waelsing   was widely renowned
most hailed of heroes   after Heremod fell
stumbled to his death   restored to Sigemund
the greater glory-name.   Good King Heremod
stooped to evil-days   shattered his kingdom
joined fiend-creatures   fared to hell with them
after his deathfall.   Danes mourned for that
bowed to anguish   baleful life-sorrow.
They ached with yearning   for those early throne-years
bountiful memories—many a wiseman
had looked to that lord   for long peace-days
feasts and friendship   as his father's king-love
had brought to the Danes—deep treachery
darkened their gift-hall   as that dangerous man
bent down to evil.   Beowulf prevailed
Hygelac's war-thane   held to his promise
brought to all of them   bright victory.

29

They raced their mounts   measured the pathway
on the track to Heorot.   The hastening of day
shoved up the sky—soon came fugitives
from their safe night-lodgings   to see that monster-arm
920   high upon the hall.   Their hopeful king
keeper of the hoard   came from the bride-bower
marched with his house-guard   to Heorot's doorway
and his queen with him,   waiting for hope-news,
measured the hall-yard   maidens at her side.
Hrothgar spoke then   stood by the doorstep
stared above him   at the steep roof-gable
garnished with gold   and Grendel's hand:
"May thanks to the Wielder   for this wondrous sight
long be in our hearts.   Loathsome mind-pain
930   Grendel has brought me.   God brings to us
wonder after wonder   Wielder of glory.
Until this day   I dared not imagine
relief from sorrow   shame and treachery
sinful murdering   when stained with gore
this best of meadhalls   mournfully stood
empty and idle—agony and grief
gripped our heart-thoughts   with no hope for mercy
a hand to defend us   from that foul hell-monster
sorcery and death.   Through the Shaper's will
940   a visiting warrior   has vanquished in the night
this murdering sprite   that no Spear-Dane's war-strength
could banish or harm.   That heartstrong woman
mother of this man   marked by the Wielder
to bear such a son   may say to the world
that the old Measurer   honored her womb-seed
blessed her in childbirth.   I choose you now
beloved Beowulf   best among warriors
as the son of my hopes—hold this kinship

near to your heart—you will never be poor
950 in goods of this world   while I wield this goldhoard.
I have often allowed   to lesser warriors
weaker in battle-strength   bounteous rewards
for smaller victories.   You've assured it now
through your great courage   that glory will be yours
forever and always.   May the almighty King
reward you for this   with wisdom and strength."
Beowulf answered   Ecgtheow's son:
"With war-willing hearts   we waited for terror
gambled our lives   gave up to murder
960 a thane of Hygelac.   I hoped as I struggled
that you for yourself   might see that monster
in all his strangeness   stripped of his life.
I hoped to bind him   hard in my grasp
clamp his fiend-corpse   to a cold slaughter-bed
hold in my handgrip   his hateful life-core
bring you his death—but his body betrayed me.
I could not hold him   here by the gift-throne
hard as I tried   when the high Measurer
planned differently—he pulled too strongly
970 fled with his life.   But he left his hand
to mark our struggle   his mighty fiend-claws
and death-wrenched shoulder.   No safety from revenge
did he buy with that bargain   no booty from hell—
not long will he live   loveless murderer
laboring in sin   for sorrow has him
clamped in a life-grip   lashed to his crimes
in baleful death-bonds—he will bide in misery
stained with hall-blood   stand for judgment
bound to the will   of the bright Measurer."
980 Then old Ecglaf's son   Unferth the heckler
stood silent there   stunned by that trophy
hushed with horror   humbled orator.

31

They stared at that hand   by the high roof-gable
terror-warped fingers—the tips of the nails
were hard as smith-steel   sharp death-talons
heathen's handspurs   a hellish warrior's
sword-tips of evil.   They all agreed there
that the best of blades   battle-swords of old
could not hew that arm   from its huge shoulder
990   hack from its body   that hell-fiend's claw-hand.

Soon it was time   to restore the meadhall
shape it for feasting—they flocked then to Heorot
warriors and women   worked through the day
washed the gore-tracks.   Golden tapestries
were hung on the walls   wondrous designs
elvishly woven   for the eyes of men.
In that bright meadhall   benches were shattered
beams unanchored   iron-hard hinges
wrenched and twisted—the roof only
1000   kept to its shape   when that shambling killer
fled to the moors   marked with a death-wound
lifeblood draining.   Nor is death avoided
not easily tricked   try it as we may
but each soul-bearer   must seek in the end
by fate impelled   a final slumber-bed—
each earth-dweller   earns a resting-place
where his body will lie   bowered from sky-light
sleeping after banquet.   Soon it was ready—
to the hall he went   Healfdene's son
1010   ready for feasting   firelight and peace.
Never have I heard   of happier warriors
more highly behaved   with their hoard-guardian.
They bent to the benches   by bright fire-flicker
lifted their cups.   Comrades together
Hrothgar and Hrothulf   hoisted their mead-drink

uncle and nephew   honored by them all
no guile in their hearts.   Heorot was filled then
with family and friends—no feuding in the air
darkened the Danes   no deep treachery.
1020 To Beowulf then   bountiful Hrothgar
gave a golden banner   beacon of victory
with bright battle-dress   breast-coat and helmet.
To the Geat came next   a great treasure-sword
borne to his hands.   To Beowulf at last
an ale-cup was served.   No shameful gifts
were laid before him   for his friends to see—
I have not yet heard   of a handsomer reward
four such treasures   trimmed well with gold
brought with such grace   to a guest in Heorot.
1030 On the helmet's crown   a hammer-hard ridge
wound with steel-wire   stood against blade-bites
a fire-tempered tube   to toughen the head-guard—
no file-sharp edges   would eat through that crown
when shielded swordmen   stepped into battle.
Then the king of the Danes   called for attention—
eight fine horses   entered the meadhall
with gold-laced bridles.   On the best was mounted
a silver saddle   studded with garnets
the gleaming battle-seat   of gladman Hrothgar
1040 when that son of Healfdene   sallied to warplay
rode before his men   to the rush of swordswings—
he was always in front   when they fell around him.
To Beowulf then   the Battle-Danes' leader
offered all of it   urged him to take
weapons and horses   hold and use them.
With royal manners   the mighty Dane-lord
guardian of that hoard   gave from his treasure
horses and weapons   worthy of his kingdom—
no courteous man   could quarrel with those gifts.

1050 Each of the Geats   every man of them
      who crossed with Beowulf   the curling sea-road
      was worthied with gifts   by the wise old king
      honored with heirlooms—then he offered wergild
      gold for that wretch   ravaged by Grendel
      viciously murdered—as more would have been
      had not God in his wisdom   and one man's courage
      withstood wyrd there.   The Wielder controlled
      all of mankind   as he always does.
      Forethought is best   future in the mind
1060 plans for everything.   All who are given
      loan-days in this world   life before darkness
      will suffer and enjoy   sorrow and happiness.

AT THIS POINT Hrothgar's minstrel celebrates Beowulf's victory with a
highly allusive episode recounting an earlier fight between Danes and
Frisians which he calls the *Freswael* ("Frisian slaughter"). A fragment of
a heroic poem about half the length of this episode, printed in 1705 from
a manuscript leaf now lost, gives Finnsburuh as the site of the battle.
Those two accounts are the only extant versions of an obviously well-
known story that has engaged *Beowulf* scholars for more than a century.
From a wilderness of versions, drawing upon both episode and fragment,
I summarize as follows:

A Danish king Hoc has two children, Hnaef and his sister, Hildeburh,
who marries Finn Folcwalding, king of the Frisians. Hnaef and sixty
retainers visit Hildeburh at Finnsburuh in Frisia. For some reason, the
Frisians attack the Danes at dawn in the hall assigned to them and fight for
five days with many Frisian casualties (including Hildeburh's son) but no
Danish dead until Hnaef is finally killed, leaving the Frisian forces badly
depleted and unable to vanquish the beleaguered Danes.

As winter approaches, a truce is made between Finn and Hengest (now
in charge of the Danes), giving the Danes an honored place in Finn's hall
and equal status with the Frisians, Finn paying wergild for Hnaef and stag-
ing a formal cremation for dead warriors, including Hnaef and his nephew,
Hildeburh's son. Some Frisians apparently return to their homes, and
Hengest spends an unhappy winter at Finnsburuh, his thoughts turning to

vengeance with the coming of spring. Hunlafing (encouraged by Guthlaf and Oslaf) gives Hengest a sword to urge him on. The Danes attack and kill Finn, loot Finnsburuh, then carry Hildeburh back to Denmark.

Then sweet strumming   silenced the company
harpstrings sounded   for Healfdene's son
fingers drew notes   found story-words
hushed mead-benches   when Hrothgar's minstrel
mourned a winter-tale   matched it with song
of the house of Finn   that fatal night-visit
when that Half-Danes' warrior   Hnaef the Scylding
1070   fell to death-rest   in Frisian slaughter.
Nor was Hildeburh's   heart rewarded
by that hostile truce—tormented queen
bereft of loved ones   by linden-shield play
her brother and son   slain in treachery
by deep spear-bites—dark was her mourning.
With heavy heart-thoughts   Hoc's daughter-child
measured destiny   when darkness paled
when the graylight sky   spread before her eyes
black murder-bale.   Battle-slaughter won
1080   fetched from life-breath   Finn's warrior-thanes
all but a few—ended at last
when Hengest and his men   held against them all—
nothing could flush them   fighting was stalled
with ominous silence—at the end of slaughter
was no victory.   They vowed peace-terms—
to Danes was offered   their own winter-home
hall-room and high-seat   to hold peacefully
with half of everything   enemies together—
before the gift-throne   Folcwalda's son
1090   would honor the Danes   each day and night-time
welcome with rings   warriors of Hengest
give from his treasure-hoard   gold arm-bracelets

in full friendship   with Frisians around them
equal in boasting   beer-cups and song.
So they swore together   solemn companions
a firm peace-pact.   Finn gave to Hengest
in full hall-council   hard oath-bindings
with his elders' advice: In honorable plenty
he would hold them all—no envious hall-thane
1100 with words or with deeds   would damage that peace
no Dane would lament   with malice on his tongue
that they now followed   forced by that truce
their lord's life-taker   through the long winter—
if one Frisian   with foul hate-words
mindful of mischief   should mention battle-thoughts
a sharp swordedge   would silence that tongue.
Oaths were honored   old gold-treasures
brought from the hoard.   The best warrior
lord of the War-Danes   was laid upon the pyre.
1110 Heaped on the balefire   battle-gear waited
bloodstained corselets   cloven mask-helmets
gilded with boar-heads   grim slaughter-guards
with too many warriors   wounded to rest.
Then came Hildeburh   where Hnaef lay waiting
bade that her son   be swallowed by flames
next to her brother   nephew by his side
at his uncle's shoulder—she sang in her grief
a keen sorrow-song   as they settled him there.
The great slaughter-fire   circled to the sky
1120 reared to the heavens.   Heads melted there
sword-woundings burst   blood sprang from them
fire-bitten bodies.   Flames swallowed all
greediest of spirits   sucked them away
the Finns and the Danes—fled was their glory.
Frisians grew restive   bereft of friends
some took winter-leave   sought their blood-kin

homes and meadhalls.   Hengest remained
suffering with Finn   a slaughter-stained winter
dreaming of release—he longed for Denmark
1130   though he dared not sail   on the surging waters
his ring-prowed ship.   The sea howled at him
wailing with storm-wind—winter locked the waves
in icy bindings   till the earth welcomed
a young new-year   as it yet calls forth
the altered seasons   always beckoning
glory-bright weather.   Then winter was gone
fair was the earth-bosom.   The exile yearned
guest to be gone.   Grief and vengeance
stronger than escape   seethed in his heart-blood—
1140   a final meeting   formed in his mind
memory of malice   moved him to stay.
He did not reject   that gesture then
when Hunlafing bore him   a bright vengeance-sword
bore to his bosom   that best of warblades—
its edges were known   to all around him.
Once more to Finn   Frisian war-king
came anxious swordbale   in his own homeland
when Guthlaf and Oslaf   with grim memories
spoke of their sorrows   that sea-voyage to death
1150   woeful winter-grief.   No wavering heart
they found in Hengest.   The hall grew red
with Frisian blood-wounds—Finn perished there
king with his men   and his queen was taken.
To their broad ship then   the Shield-Danes bore
whatever they found   in Finn's meadhall
stripped it of swords   secret treasure-hoard
wondrous gemstones.   On the welling sea
they ferried his wife   to family in Denmark
safe with her kin.

                    The song was ended

1160   the gleeman's tale.   It was time for joy
    bench-laughter brightened   bearers brought forth
    wine in wonder-cups.   Then Wealhtheow approached
    with gold-gleaming neck-ring   where nephew and king
    feasted in friendship   yet faithful as kin.
    There was Unferth the heckler   at Hrothgar's feet—
    they held him in trust   hailed his courage
    though to his family   he failed in honor
    at clashing of swordedge.   The queen spoke then:
    "Take this cupful   my king and husband
1170   treasure-sharing lord.   Look to happiness
    gold-friend to men—to these Geats offer
    welcoming words   as a wise man should.
    Be glad with these Geats   give of that treasure
    fetched to your goldhoard   from far and from near.
    I have heard men say   you would have for a son
    that hero among them.   Heorot is purged
    this bright wine-hall.   Wield while you can
    these fine riches   and to family bequeath
    this land and kingdom   when you leave this world
1180   to seek your destiny.   I am sure that Hrothulf
    our kind brother-son   will care for our young ones
    guide and hold them   if you go before him
    give up this world   in your waning years.
    He will surely repay us   shelter our sons
    if he well remembers   how we watched over him
    held him as our own   gave help in everything
    shepherded our kin   through a safe childhood."
    She turned to the benches   where her boys were sitting
    Hrethric and Hrothmund   and a host of young ones
1190   the youth together—there the good one sat
    Beowulf the Geat   by the brothers' side.

HAVING PUBLICLY REMINDED HROTHULF of his duty to her two young sons—as she later solicits Beowulf's help with them—Wealhtheow turns to where they sit with Beowulf and presents him with further rewards, including a gold neck-ring compared by the *Beowulf* poet with the legendary Brosinga necklace in one of his briefest and most obscure allusions. Drawing upon both history and legend, we may think of Hama as having stolen this great collar or torque from Eormenric (the historic Gothic king Ermanaric) and carried it to the "bright city" where he chose "eternal glory"—probably a reference to his acceptance of Christianity. We then have the first of several references to Hygelac's later invasion of the lower Rhine, where he is killed. Though Beowulf later presents this neck-ring to Hygd, the poet here says that Hygelac wore it on his fatal expedition.

> A cup was offered   in kind friendship
> with terms of welcome   then twisted gold
> placed before him   a pair of arm-bracelets
> corselets and garments   with the greatest neck-ring
> of all on this earth   that ever I heard of.
> No tales have told   of a treasure so rich
> a finer hoard-ring   since Hama bore away
> to that bright citadel   the Brosinga necklace,
1200 > famed gold-marvel,   fled with that treasure
> from Eormenric's torment   to eternal glory.
> That hoard-ring was borne   by Hygelac the Geat
> Swerting's nephew   when he sailed from home
> led a plunder-raid   on his last seafaring
> fought for war-booty.   Wyrd took him then
> when boasting with pride   he brought to all of them
> death among Frisians.   He ferried that treasure
> studded with gemstones   over seething wave-rolls
> fated king-warrior—he fell beneath his shield.
1210 > To the Franks he left   his lifeless body
> gold-laced mailcoat   and glorious neck-ring.

Then lesser warriors   looted that treasure
as he lay battle-shorn   lord of the Geats—
he paid for that pride.
                                Applause filled the hall
as Wealhtheow spoke   stood before her guest:
"Have luck with this neck-ring   beloved Beowulf
accept these gifts   gold-gleaming treasures
and use them well—may you win always
make known your strength   and save for these boys
1220   wise counsel-words—I'll reward you for that.
You have earned such fame   that from far and near
in this wide middle-earth   men will honor you
as far as the sea   circles this windyard
these high cliffwalls.   Keep while you live
peace with your courage.   I'll repay you for that
with bright treasure-gifts.   Be to my sons
a gentle hero   with joy in your heart.
Each man at this feast   is faithful to all
loyal to his lord   loving in mindthoughts—
1230   these thanes are together   good men and strong
these drunken warriors   do as I bid them."
She sat then to banquet   the best of feasting
warmed with wine-cups—warriors rejoiced
unwary of their fate   waiting for destiny
like friends before them   at failing of day
when Hrothgar left them   to lie in his bower
went to his rest.   War-Danes guarded
the darkening meadhall   as in days gone by.
They cleared the bench-planks,   brought for sleeprest
1240   bedding and bolsters.   A beer-drinker there
ready for his doom   rested among them.
They set by their heads   where hands could reach them
bright linden-shields—on benches above them
over sleeping warriors   weapons were ready

40

hard mask-helmets   hand-locked corselets
stout-shafted spears.   They were seldom caught
unready for war   waking or sleeping
at home or afield   held themselves ready
for their lord's command   moments of swordplay
1250   their war-sovereign's needs—they were worthy men.

II

They sank to their sleep.   One sorely paid
for his evening slumber   like others before him
since Grendel came to them   greedy hall-watcher
rage in his blood   till he blundered at last
death came to him.   The Danes discovered
that one still living   waited for that night
slouched through the shadows   searching for revenge
grim murder-fiend—Grendel's hell-mother
bereaved monster-wife   mourned for her child.
1260   She was damned to hide   in a dark water-home
cold wildwood stream   since Cain murdered
his only brother-kin   beat down to earth
his father's son-child.   He was sent for that
marked with murder   from man's company
banished to wasteland.   Then woke from his loins
misbegotten monsters.   Among them was Grendel
hate-hearted fiend   who found at Heorot
a waking strength-warrior   waiting in that hall.
Grendel grabbed him   grappled his hand—
1270   but mindful of power   the mercy of his strength
that bountiful gift   from God's kingdom
the warrior caught him   clamped in his fingers
that great claw-hand   crushed that night-killer
gripped him to death.   Grendel went slinking
crossed the moorland   to his cold death-cavern

41

exiled from mercy.   Then his mother sorrowed
grieved for her child   greedy for man-blood
went prowling for vengeance   payment for her son.
She came then to Heorot   where careless Shield-Danes
1280   slumbered peacefully.   They soon found there
the old night-torture   when in through the door
came Grendel's mother.   Her great warrior-strength
was less than her son's   as little as a woman's
is weaker in warfare   than a weaponed man's
when bloodied swordblades   smith-hammered edges
slash helmet-crowns   hard over boar-crests
gold-handled swords   shear against mask-helmets.
Sleeping warriors   woke to the fight
reached for swordblades   raised linden-shields
1290   hoisted their weapons—helmets and corselets
were left by the benches   in that lunging raid.
She yearned to leave them   longed to be away
flee with her life   when they found her there—
quickly she snared   a single warrior
fastened in her claws   as she fled to the moor.
That ill-fated Dane   was dearest to Hrothgar
of all warriors   in that wide kingdom
powerful shieldman   snatched from his rest
battle-worthy thane.   Nor was Beowulf there
1300   who slept through the night   in a separate bower
champion of the Geats   with his great treasures.
Sorrow came to Heorot—she snatched from the gable
that high-hung monster-arm—horror came back then
to the wakening death-hall.   It was woeful bargaining
each party to pay   the price of slaughter
with a loved-one's life.

That forlorn treasure-king
sorrow-wounded lord   sang a mourning-song
grieved for his heart-thane   hearth-friend and warrior

42

a king's counselor   killed in his hall.
1310   Quickly was Beowulf   battle-worn visitor
called to his bower.   At breaking of day
he went with his shieldmen   walked through the dawn
to the king's rest house—that bereft throne-warden
wondered in misery   if the Wielder of us all
ever would spare them   save them from fiendgrief.
Then Hygelac's thane   with hand-chosen warriors
crossed the floor-planks   clinked an armor-song
stood before the king   sorrowing Dane-lord
asked if his night-rest   had eased his suffering
1320   if the breaking of Grendel   had brought peace to him.
Hrothgar answered   helm of the Shield-Danes:
"Don't ask about happiness!   Horror has returned
to the Danes in Heorot.   Dead is Aeschere
good Yrmenlaf's   guide and blood-brother
my closest adviser   counsel to us all
shoulder-companion   when shields were hoisted
defender of my life   when foot-warriors clashed
helmets were swordstruck.   So should a man be
always beside us   as Aeschere was!
1330   He found in Heorot   a hell-spawned murderer
restless hand-killer.   From our high meadhall
that slaughter-stained spirit   has sought her corpse-cave
I know not where.   She now has avenged
the felling of Grendel   that feud you began
with violent grappling   that great handgrip
that settled our account   for those cold death-years
the closing of Heorot.   He cringed at your hand
went dying through the night   and now this she-fiend
has avenged her monster-son   vicious man-killer—
1340   too far she has carried   this feud over blood-kin
it seems to us all   aching in our minds
weeping for Aeschere   warrior of my heart

43

high-minded hall-thane—now his hand is idle
that once granted us   each wish and command.
I have heard evening-tales   hearth-talk of scouts
of hall-messengers   hailing from abroad
that they have sighted   a solitary pair
monstrous moor-walkers   moving through shadows
sorrowful fen-spirits.   They say that one of them
1350 misshapen exile   is most like a woman—
the wanderer with her   woefully deformed
prowled the march-tracks   manlike to their eyes
yet bigger by far   than the best of warriors.
In times long past   tenders of the land
named him Grendel.   No one can say
what creatures spawned them   their kin in this world.
They live secretly   in a shadowy land
dwell by wolf-slopes   wind-tortured bluffs
gloomy fen-hollows   where a forested stream
1360 dives from the bluffs   down past earthlight
flows underground.   Not far from Heorot
measured in miles   the mere lies hidden—
reaching above it   with rime-covered branches
strong-rooted trees   stretch from rock-slopes.
At night may be seen   a strange wonder-sight
fire on the water.   No wiseman lives
who knows the bottom   of that black monster-home.
Though the heath-prancer   by hounds labored
the strong-antlered hart   may seek life-haven
1370 driven from afar   he will die beside it
forfeit his life there   for fear of crossing
plunging his head   in that hell-cursed water.
A surging of waves   swirls to the clouds
when whistling winds   come whirling in anger
to that sorrowful place—the sky hangs gloomy
and the heavens weep.   Our hope for mercy

lies only in your help.   The home of these fiends
dark moor-cavern   monsters' water-den
is not far from Heorot.   Find it if you dare!
1380   I will reward you   with weapons and gold
ancient treasure-gifts   as I earlier did
linked mail-corselets   if you live to return."
Beowulf spoke   son of Ecgtheow:
"Do not grieve, old battle-king!   It is better for all
to fight for our friends   than fall into mourning.
Each one among us   shall mark the end
of this worldly life.   Let him who may
earn deeds of glory   before death takes him—
after life-days   honor-fame is best.
1390   Arise, good guardian   let us go quickly
to find the moor-tracks   of that murdering fiend.
I promise you firmly   she will find no safety
in the earth's caverns   or the cold forest-mounds—
nowhere in this land   will she live for long!
At this painful dawning   have patience with sorrow
bear your death-grief   in your deep-wounded heart."
Up stood the king   called to his God then
thanked him for the words   that warrior had spoken.
Then for Hrothgar   a horse was saddled
1400   curly-maned war-steed.   The wise Dane-leader
went forth in splendor.   Warriors advanced
marched from the hall.   The monstrous tracks
were easy to follow   on the forest-narrow path
where that loveless creature   loped through the trees
over wild moorland   wandering streams
bearing that body   the best counsel-thane
of all who with Hrothgar   made Heorot their home.
The lord of the Danes   led through wilderness
steep stone-passes   solitary trails
1410   narrow-dark gorges   unknown trackways

slippery rockbluffs   secret demon-dens.
He rode before them   following the signs
guided his warriors   Geats with the Danes
till suddenly they found   frosted tree-branches
stretching mournfully   over sloping grayrock
joyless treelimbs   over trembling water
dreary and wind-driven.   Danes were silent
with sorrow in their hearts   at the sight before them
when they circled the mere   saw greeting them
1420   on the moldering bank   of that bloodstained water
on the edge of that hell-sump   Aeschere's head.
The water-top heaved   as they hovered around it
with hot gore-swells.   Horn-notes sounded
a strong battle-song.   They sat by the bank.
In that hell-murky mere   many a snake-creature
curious water-worms   cut through the gore—
on the hard bank-slopes   black fiends were roiling
serpents and mere-sprites   slid along the rock—
by cold morninglight   they moved through the water
1430   slithering with greed.   They scattered then in anger
bitter and blood-swelled   as the bright horn-notes
signaled a challenge.   The chief of the Geats
sent from a yew-bow   a sharp arrowhead
struck to the life-core   a loathsome mere-creature
ended its misery—it afterwards became
a lazier swimmer   when its life departed.
With a barbed boar-spear   it was brought to shore
hooked with steel-teeth   hauled to the edge
rolled on the rockbank   robbed of lifeblood—
1440   they gazed in wonder   at that grisly swim-serpent
blackening with death.
                                    Then Beowulf prepared
called for his armor   careless of his life.
Bright warrior-mail   bonded by hands

linked armor-coat   locked against swordswings
covered his breastcage   enclosed his heart
that no fiendgrip   might fix upon his life
grapple to his soul   with grim hell-fingers.
A gleaming mask-helmet   guarded his head
gilded with boar-crests   bordering the rim
1450   old treasure-helm   ancient wonder-smith's
shield against steel-bites   that no sharp blade-edge
might slice through to him   as he sought the mere-ground
stroked to the bottom   of that baleful pond
wrapped against death   in rich armor-bonds.
Nor was it the worst   of weapons that day
that Unferth loaned him   orator of Heorot—
a hard cutting-sword   Hrunting by name
praised through the years   by proud weapon-thanes.
The hammer-forged blade   of hand-twisted steelbands
1460   was hardened by blood—the bite of its edges
had never yet failed   a firm-handed warrior
anyone who dared   death in battle-rush—
its strength was known   in stories of war-clash
when edges and spearshafts   sang through the air.
That son of Ecglaf   strong counsel-thane
offered no charges   no challenging wine-words
when he loaned his battle-blade   by that blood-red mere
to the better sword-champion—though brave in memory
he dared not dive   in that deep hell-water
1470   to foster his fame—he forfeited there
stories of his past.   The proud guest-warrior
was ready now for all   eager for that fight.
Beowulf spoke   son of Ecgtheow:
"Beloved Hrothgar   Healfdene's son
remember your words   in the warmth of Heorot
before I go swimming   in search of this monster—
if ever I serve you   in your hour of need

and part with my life-breath   you have promised to be
for me and my folk-thanes   a father to my name.
1480   Let your good hand   harbor my shield-thanes
my board-companions   if battle takes my life
and send to Hygelac,   Hrothgar my lord,
those marvelous treasures   that you made my own.
He will learn from that gold,   the Geats' hall-king
good son of Hrethel,   when he sees those rewards,
that I found in Denmark   a fine goldwarden
proud ring-giver   and prospered while I lived.
Give to Unferth   my good treasure-sword
twist-hammered blade   bound by steel-smiths
1490   a man's war-weapon.   I will manage with Hrunting
earn my goldgifts   or enter into death."
After those words   the Weather-Geats' leader
turned to his work—no time would he waste
for answering speech—the shivering water
swallowed him away.   It was wondrously long
before handstrokes bore him   to the bottom of that mere.
Soon that water-fiend   warden of the depths
guardian of fury   through fifty murder-years
found an alien creature   come to explore
1500   from the earth above her   that bleak hell-home.
She grabbed him then   with her great handspurs
clenched him with her claws—the covering mailcoat
linked corselet-rings   locked with steelmesh
stopped those talons   from stabbing his heart—
those loathsome fingers   failed against smith-hands.
That black she-wolf   bore him away
tugged through the water   that warrior from above
to her deep cavern-den—caught in that grasp
he could wield no weapons—wondrous creatures
1510   pressed around him   reached for his life
crunched with nail-teeth   gnashed at his breast-coat

greedy for his blood.   Then that grim wolf-woman
dragged him to her cave   cold rock-chamber—
no roiling water   could reach to that den
roofed against flood-water   far beneath the earth—
firelight shimmered there   on the floor of that dungeon
restless flame-shadows   flickered on the wall.
Now he could see her   sorrowful blood-fiend
great mere-monster—he grabbed his sword then
1520   swung high with it   swept it down at her
struck at the head   with a sounding blade-tone
steel-song ringing.   He soon discovered
that his bright swordedge   could not bite that flesh
strike to that life—that strong treasure-sword
failed him at need.   Those file-hard edges
had cut through battle-mail   in countless shield-fights
sheared through mask-helmets—that marvelous
        war-weapon
had never forfeited   the fame of its past.
Beowulf remembered   boastwords in Heorot
1530   Hygelac's hearth-thane   held to his promise—
he flung the sword then   far across the cave
flushed with anger   no failure in his heart—
he remembered his handgrasp   mindful of Grendel
his great gripstrength.   A good war-thane
fighting for fame   following name-glory
will trust his courage   no care for his life.
He grabbed her then   Grendel's hell-mother
grappled her shoulders   in his great handvice
tugged at her arms   with angry heartstrength
1540   twisted her backwards   bent her to the floor.
She clamped his arms   in her cold fiendgrip
returned his tugging   with tight claw-fingers—
she toppled him over   with towering strength
raging with fire-eyes   felled him to the floor

leapt on his chest   lifted her shortsword
broad murder-knife   burning to avenge
her only offspring.   Over his breastcage
a hand-locked mailcoat   harbored his life
countered the piercing   of point and edge.
1550 He would soon have died there   deep under the earth
Ecgtheow's son   strong Geat-champion
but his hard battle-coat   held against that thrust—
close-woven steelmesh   clenched against swordbite
kept him from death—the Deemer of this world
decided that contest   the Shaper of mankind
strengthened that warrior   as he stood to his feet.
He saw then glittering   a great hoard-weapon
smith-wrought by giants   a sword for victory
blade for a champion   best of war-weapons
1560 gleaming with goldwork   greater in steel-weight
than any other man   could manage in warfare.
He seized it by the hilt,   Shield-Danes' hall-guest,
grasped in his hands   the gold-gleaming handle
raised it in anger   rage in his heart
swung it at her neck   with his strong handgrip
till it bit through the flesh   burst fiend-muscles
broke through bone-rings—the blade cut through
felled her to the floor   fated hell-creature—
the sword was blooded   and Beowulf rejoiced.
1570 Light came rushing   radiant and warm
as God's bright candle   glows in the heavens
glittering above.   He gazed about him
moved along the wall   wielding his giant-sword
with a great hilt-grip,   Hygelac's shield-thane
towering with rage—yet ready for vengeance
he stepped through the cavern   searched for Grendel
anxious to repay   that prowling visitor
for years of torture   in that tall meadhall

twelve long winters   of woeful murder
1580   when he fell upon Hrothgar's   hearth-companions
slew them in their sleep   swallowed them down,
fifteen warriors   of the folk of Denmark,
and carried from the hall   to his cold water-den
the same number.   He saw him then
Grendel lying there   with a gaping shoulder-wound
wearied by his crimes   waiting for judgment
lifeless at last   after long murder-years
horror in Heorot.   With a hard swordswing
Beowulf slashed at him   struck through his neck
1590   ended that hall-feud   for Healfdene's son.

Watching at the mere-top   the waiting Shield-Danes
Hrothgar's counselors   cold in their hearts
saw a welling of blood   waves of death-gore
rise to the surface.   Sorrowful advisers
battle-weary hall-thanes   borne down by grief
carried to their king   a care-heavy message—
they hoped no longer   that the leader of the Geats
might rise in victory   through that roiling water
return to his men—they murmured in sorrow
1600   grieved that the she-wolf   had slaughtered him below.
The sun swung low.   They left the mere then—
those mourning Shield-Danes   sought with their king
their good meadhall.   Their guests stayed on
sick with horror   stared at the blood-froth.
They wished without hope   that their hero would surface
dive up to them.   Deep below the earth
that broad wonder-blade   wasted and quivered
withered in that blood—it wavered and dripped
melted and shrunk   like sun-warmed icicles
1610   when the Ruler of heaven   unwraps frost-bindings
unwinds water-ropes,   Wielder of us all,

of times and seasons   the true Measurer.
The lord of the Geats   looked at the treasures
heaped and glittering   in that grisly fiend-hall—
from the wealth before him   he wanted no more
than Grendel's head   and that golden swordhilt—
the blade had vanished   burned down to nothing
melted in the heat   of that hell-spirit's blood.
Soon he was swimming   straight up to earthlight
1620   shot through the surface   of that seething mere.
That peaceful pond   was purged of evil
opened to sunlight   when those alien spirits
paid for their loan-days   with their pitiful lives.
He came then to land   leader of the Geats
proud of the booty   he bore in his hands
great hell-mysteries   haled from the depths.
His thanes received him   thankful to their God
for bringing him back   from that baleful journey
safe after his fight   with that sorceress of death.
1630   His hard mask-helmet   hand-woven corselet
were quickly removed.   The mere grew quiet
calm monster-pond   colored with fiend-blood.
They left that devil's hole   led by their champion,
no mourning in their minds,   measured the trackways
the known moorpaths.   Marching Geat-thanes
bore the great head,   grim death-plunder,
climbed through the mist   past the cold rockstream
followed the pathway—four good warriors
bore on their spearshafts,   struggling with the weight,
1640   Grendel's monster-head   through green forest-trees.
Fourteen spear-fighters   filed across the meadow
marched upon the hall   with its high gold-gables
Geats all together—their good warleader
towered among them   trod the meadowgrass.
Once more he approached   the proud wine-hall

champion of the Geats   chosen for battle-fame
to hail the king there   Hrothgar the Dane.
Hefted by the hair   the head of that murderer
was borne into the hall   where beer-drinkers waited—
1650 Shield-Danes gathered there   with their good hall-queen
to gaze upon that marvel   that great monster-head.
Beowulf spoke   son of Ecgtheow:
"From Grendel's mere,   gladman Hrothgar
bountiful lord,   we bring gifts to you
tokens of victory   tidings of relief.
I barely endured   that deep monster-fight
under dark blood-water   where death came pressing
stabbing at my heart—I would still be there
if the great Shaper   had not shielded my life.
1660 No help was Hrunting   with hell's sorcery
that battle-sharpened blade   could not bite
        monster-flesh—
then the great Wielder   Glory-King of all
gave me a wonder-blade   granted to my sight
a huge giant-sword   hanging by the wall.
I reached for the hilt   raised it quickly
slashed at that she-wolf   sliced through her neck
ended her misery.   Then that mighty wonder-blade
burned and dwindled   dark monster-blood
melted it away.   This marvelous swordhilt
1670 I bring back to you.   Both man-killers
are banished from Heorot   hall of the Danes.
I promise you this night,   proud land-master,
you may sleep soundly   sorrowing no more.
All of your warriors   women and children
youth and elders   aged counselors
all of your Shield-Danes   may slumber in peace
reprieved from night-murder   prowling thane-killers."
Then that ancient swordhilt   shining with old-gold

strange work of giants   wonder-smith's pattern
1680 was placed in the hands   of Healfdene's son—
after long winters   longing for mercy
with nightbale and tears   terror was sleeping.
Those murdering moor-stalkers   mother and fiend-son
kept to their cavern   under cold forest-stream.
That old treasure-hilt   ancient wonderwork
came into the hands   of Heorot's treasure-king
the best battle-lord   in the breadth of Denmark.
Hrothgar was gladdened   gazed upon the hilt
curious sword-handle—cut into the gold
1690 was a tale of evil   that old earth-struggle
when great flood-waters   fell upon earth-giants
carried them away—the Wielder of all
God of creation   crushed their wickedness
with welling water-rush   washed them from earth.
Written in rune-marks   on that rich swordhilt,
gleaming goldplate   garnished with serpents,
was a curious name   who caused that sword
to be shaped and hammered   smithied in yoredays
a weapon for the mighty.   Then the wise Dane-lord
1700 Healfdene's son   spoke his mindthoughts:
"It can well be said   by sons of this earth
by those who remember   moments of the past,
clashing of spearshields   that this keen battle-thane
was born for glory!   Beowulf my friend
your fame is founded   far across the waves
where wise men gather.   Guard it carefully
strength with wisdom.   I will stand by my word
make good my promises.   To your Geat-friends now
you will come with counsel   courage for their hearts
through long comfort-years.
1710   Not so kind was Heremod
to the kin of Ecgwela   care-heavy Shield-Danes—

he brought them no joy   but baleful murder
dark death-sorrows   to his Danish followers.
With hot rage-thoughts   he ravaged his people
hearth-companions   till hate severed him,
jealous slaughter-king,   from the joys of men
though the great Measurer   marked him for honor
lifted him on high   haled him to a throne
a towering meadhall.   To his mind came rushing
1720   blood-hungry thoughts—no bracelets or rings
he gave to his warriors   but woeful misery
suffering and sorrow   sharp death-grieving
endless murder-bale.   Mark carefully
this lesson of anguish—old in winters
I warn you by this.   It is wondrous to see
how almighty God   in his endless wisdom
grants unto a man   a mind to rule with
kingdom and meadhall   to keep until death.
At times the Measurer   maker of us all
1730   brings moments of pleasure   to those proud
              man-thoughts
gives to that war-king   worldly power-goods
hall and homeland   to hold for his own
renders him ruler   of regions of the earth
a broad kingdom—he cannot foresee
in his own unwisdom   an end to such wealth.
He dwells in happiness   no hindrance bothers him
no illness or age   or evil reckoning
darkens his mind   no deep serpent-thoughts
edge-hate in his heart—but all this loan-world
1740   bends to his will   welcomes him with gold
till high throne-thoughts   throng into his mind
gather in his head.   Then the guardian sleeps
the soul's warden—it slumbers too long
while a silent slayer   slips close to him

shoots from his bow   baleful arrows.
Deep into his heart   hard under shield-guard
strikes the arrowhead—no armor withstands
that quiet marksman   cold mind-killer.
What he long has held   too little contents him
1750 greed grapples him   he gives no longer
gold-patterned rings   reckons no ending
of borrowed treasure-years   bright earth-fortune
granted by God   the great Measurer.
The last of splendor   slips into darkness
that loaned king-body   cracks upon the pyre
swirls away in smoke—soon another one
steps to the gift-throne   shares his goldhoard
turns that treachery   to trust and reward.
Guard against life-bale   beloved Beowulf
1760 best of warriors   and win for your soul
eternal counsel—do not care for pride
great shield-champion!   The glory of your strength
lasts for a while   but not long after
sickness or spear-point   will sever you from life
or the fire's embrace   or the flood's welling
or the file-hard sword   or the flight of a spear
or bane-bearing age—the brightness of your eye
will dim and darken.   Destiny is waiting
and death will take you   down into the earth.
1770 I have held the Shield-Danes   for half a century
ruled them under heaven   harbored them from war
against many a people   on this proud earthyard—
no enemy to peace   asking for bloodshed
spearshaft or swordedge   for settlement of feuds.
Then in my homeland   happiness departed
joy turned to sorrow   when jealous-mad Grendel
careless murderer   came into my hall—
through long winters   I leaned on my sorrow

a breaking of my mind.   To the bright Measurer
1780 thanks for deliverance   from long heartache,
for this swordstruck head   severed from that murderer
this grim death-trophy   through the Deemer's mercy.
But sit now to banquet   songs and ale-cups
with your hearth-companions.   By peaceful morninglight
goldgifts will travel   from my treasure to you."
Beowulf was gladdened   by those bountiful words
sat by the gift-throne   with his Geats around him.
Bright bench-laughter   bore to the rafters
sounds of victory   servants brought ale-cups
1790 to Geats and to Danes.   Then dark night-shadows
loomed above the hall.   Hrothgar rose then
king of the Spear-Danes   called for night-sleep
for silence and peace.   Soon then Beowulf
yearning for bedrest   bent to his hall-bench
sank gratefully   to slumber in Heorot
once more a night-guest   in that mighty hallroom.
The Danes' thane-servant   thoughtful of their needs
spread bench-covers   bore final cupfuls
readied the meadhall   for rest in the night.
1800 The great-hearted slept   in that steep-gabled hall
tall and gold-trimmed—Geats rested there
till the black-shining raven   raised morning-gray
a lifting of darkness.   Dawnlight came shoving
bright above the shadows   scattering night-creatures.
Hygelac's thanes   hailed the sunrise
yearned for the sea   a sail to carry them
to that known headland   the hall of their king.
Their hero commanded   Hrunting to be borne
returned to Unferth   old Ecglaf's son
1810 urged him to take it—he told well of it
thanked him for the loan   of that long-famed warblade
strong warrior-steel   sharp helmet-bane

57

when good men gather   to gamble their lives.
Then sea-ready warriors   with their shining weapons
yearned to be gone.   Their good sail-skipper
stepped to the gift-throne   stood before the king—
gladman Hrothgar   hailed him once more.
Beowulf spoke   son of Ecgtheow:
"Now we Geat-thanes   guests across the sea
1820   are set for sailing   over steep wave-rolls
home to Hygelac.   Here you welcomed us
opened your goldhoard   granted us treasures.
If ever on this earth   I may earn your love
help you in sorrow   sickness or defeat
save you from slaughter   my ship will return.
If news comes to me   across the seaswell
that scurrilous neighbors   scheme for your life
trap you in Heorot   like those hell-spawned demons
I will sail back to you   bring you an army
1830   thousands of linden-shields.   My lord Hygelac
king of the Geats   kin and battle-friend
still young in winters   stands behind me—
he will back me well   when I bring help to you
a forest of spears   file-sharp warblades
a navy of shieldmen   when your need is great.
If Hrethric travels   to the home of the Geats
I promise you now   proud treasure-king
he will find friends there.   Fortune abroad
comes to the sailor   who himself prevails."
1840   Hrothgar answered   helm of the Danes:
"These stronghearted words   were sent down to you
from the high Wielder.   I have heard no man
so young in winters   so wealthy in thought.
You are strong in body   bold in mind-courage
wise within your words.   I will wager you now
if it comes to the Geats   that cold battle-death

a whining spearshaft   or sharp battle-blade
sends from this earth   that son of Hrethel—
if age or steel   strikes down your uncle
1850 leads your dear king   from these loaned earth-days
and you live after him   beloved Beowulf—
Geats will not find   a greater hall-thane
to raise to their gift-throne.   Your good mindthoughts
bring more pleasure   the more you stay with us.
You've brought to us all   to both our people
to men of the Geats   and these good Spear-Danes
peace between us   no time for warplay
anger and hatred   as in earlier days.
As long as I wield   this wide kingdom
1860 treasure-gifts will sail   from shore to shore
gold will bring greetings   to Götland from Denmark
the ring-prowed ship   will send across the waves
gifts and love-tokens.   We will live in friendship
forged against enemies   fast in loyalty
your people and mine   proud blood-brothers."
Then Hrothgar gave   to his good heart-son
twelve treasure-gifts   to that tall champion
bade him go then   to greet Hygelac
sail there in safety   with his strong prowship.
1870 Then the old battle-king   embraced his hero
clasped him in his arms   kissed him farewell
with tears of regret   for that time of parting
sweet sorrow-thoughts.   It seemed to them both
the old wiseman   and the warrior from Götland
that no more in that life   loaned by the Measurer
would they share hearth-words.   To the Shield-Danes'
      king
that young sea-warrior   was so strongly beloved
it swelled in his heart   surged with regret
that this son of Ecgtheow   would sail far from him

1880 back towards his home.   Then Beowulf left
gold-proud warrior   gladdened with treasure
measured the sea-path.   His sail was waiting
riding on anchor   ready for the sea.
The bountiful gifts   of that good Dane-lord
were praised by the men.   That proud hall-king
was blameless in all   best of warriors
till age wearied him   withered his strength.
They came to the sea   sailors from abroad
a band of warriors   bearing ring-corselets
1890 linked armor-mail.   The landwarden watched
as their burnished weapons   winked in the sun—
from the high cliff-top   he hailed all of them,
no challenge in his heart   but cheerful greeting,
rode to meet them   made them welcome
in their bright armor   back to their keel-ship.
The sand-bound vessel   soon was gift-laden
its broad board-deck   burdened with gifts
horses and treasures—the high mast towered
over Hrothgar's bounty   bright gold-treasures.
1900 To the good beach-guard   Beowulf gave then
a gold-wound sword   a gift to honor him
on the benches of Heorot   bettered by that weapon
sword for a champion.
                              The ship took wind
drove across the waves   from the Danish cliff-coast.
The sail crackled   shoved by ocean-winds
mast-ropes trembled   tight sail-anchors—
piling seaswells   pounded clinker-boards
bound for Götland—the good wave-cutter
plunged into the foam   flew with sail-wing
1910 followed the swan-road   skimmed across the sea
till headlands of home   hovered above them
the known seacliffs—shoved by the wind

the keel carried them   to calm shoresand.
The coastguard came riding   ready for beaching—
through long watch-days   he waited for their mast
gazed at the skyline   for signs of homecoming.
They roped to shoresand   the ring-prowed ship
lashed to its anchor   the lean wave-plow
safe from surf-crashing   surging water-throngs.
1920 Treasures were borne   from the broad ship-bosom
war-gear and horses.   The high meadhall
lifted its gables   by the looming seawall
where Hygelac waited   wise Hrethel's son
good treasure-king   with his Geats around him.
The hall towered there   high above the sea
where Hygd the fair one   Haereth's daughter-child
waited with her king   wise and generous
though young in winters   worthy folk-queen
made for a kingdom—no miser was she
1930 with gifts to her Geats   gold and weapons
treasure from her hands.

AT THIS POINT a nameless woman is abruptly introduced as a contrast to
Hygd and a puzzle to *Beowulf* scholars. A vicious torturer and man-killer
before marriage, she is sent "overseas" by her father to marry King Offa,
who tames her into a model queen, her progression thus being the oppo-
site of Heremod's. The abruptness of this allusion and obscurity of her
name, also the elaborate praise of Offa, have caused much speculation
about the possible spuriousness of this passage, and since two historic
kings were named Offa—the first a Continental king of the Angles in the
fourth century and the second an English king of the Mercians in the
eighth—it is impossible to determine what the *Beowulf* poet had in mind,
if indeed it is not an interpolation in honor of the Mercian king, in whose
reign some critics have suggested that the poem may have been composed.
Garmund is the father of the Continental Offa, Eomer is Offa's son, and
Hemming is their kin.

Beowulf then predicts trouble between Danes and Heathobards, which will eventually lead to the burning of Heorot foreshadowed earlier in the poem. Hoping to settle an old feud, Hrothgar has betrothed his daughter Freawaru to Ingeld, son of King Froda of the Heathobards, who was slain by Danes in battle. Beowulf, in his report to Hygelac, then imagines that an old Heathobard warrior, incensed by a young member of Freawaru's retinue who struts about wearing the sword of a slain Heathobard warrior, will urge the son of the slain warrior to take revenge, after which Ingeld will be forced to renew hostilities.

Beowulf's unpromising youth is a common folktale motif also found in a Latin life of Offa the Angle. Beowulf is granted a large landholding by Hygelac—"seven thousand," the poet says, without further specification—but in any case it is nearly half of the Geatish kingdom, though somewhat less than Hygelac's holding.

She tortured and murdered

powerful princess   proud king's daughter—
not one hall-thane   hero or servant
save the fond father   of that fearsome maid
dared look at her   by the light of day—
his hands would be locked   lashed with death-bonds
no hope for his life—that harmless crime
would soon be settled   with a sharp warblade,
slashing swordbale   would sever from life
1940   that pitiful wretch.   No peaceful lady
would torture her thanes   truss them for death
condemn to the blade   dear retainers
for imaginary insults   to her maiden honor.
Hemming's kinsman   calmed that slaughter-maid—
ale-drinkers say   that she softened hate-moments
mellowed murder-thoughts   measured her commands
since first she was given,   gold-endowed princess,
to that young champion   chosen for his queen
sent across the waves   by her sorrowing father
1950   to Offa the king   come to his meadhall
to share the gift-throne.   She soon bent to him

welcomed hall-thanes   hailed peace-offerings
used her wealth there   for young and for old.
With high love-thoughts   she held to her king
who of all mankind,   as men have told me,
was strongest of throne-men   from sandshore to
      sandshore
on the earth's broadland—Offa was spear-keen
tall thane-master   in thronging of war
stronghearted gift-king   sharing gold-treasures
1960   a shield for his homeland.   His son was Eomer
hall-worthy king-child   Hemming's kinsman
Garmund's grandson   good warrior-prince.

Over the shoresand   with his shoal of warriors
Beowulf went marching   measured the sea-rim
wide cliff-beaches.   The world-candle shone
southward to the sea.   They stepped to the path
mounted the sea-wall   where their mighty lord
Ongentheow's bane   bountiful hall-king
helm of the Geats   held his gift-throne
1970   shared his treasure-hoard.   Soon news-tidings
of Beowulf's beaching   were borne to Hygelac—
strong and treasure-proud   sailors were landsafe
home with their lives—linden-shield thanes
stepped to the hall   hailed their people-king.
Soon were benches   bared to receive them
the roomy wine-hall   ready for feasting.
The beloved sailor   sat by his king
nephew by his uncle   urged by welcome-words
glad hearth-greetings   from Hrethel's son
1980   hearthlord of the Geats.   The good peace-queen
moved throughout the hall   Haereth's daughter-child
bore among the benches   bright ale-vessels
served them with her hands.   Then Hygelac spoke

asked for news-words   from his nephew beside him
eager for tidings   of that trip to Denmark
Sea-Geats sailing   to the Shield-Danes' hall:
"What luck did you have   beloved Beowulf
when you foolishly left   on that long sea-sail
seeking adventure   over salty water
1990   monsters in Heorot?   Did you help the Danes
win for Hrothgar   a healthier meadhall
for that thane-deprived king?   My thoughts troubled me
seethed with sorrow   for that senseless voyage
a bad bargain.   I begged you to stay
ignore that fiend   foul murder-guest
to let the Shield-Danes   look to their feud
deal with Grendel.   To God I give thanks
that I see you now   sound and war-proud."
Beowulf spoke   son of Ecgtheow:
2000   "That great struggle   gladman Hygelac
is no secret now   how I shared with Grendel
a grim grip-battle   in that great meadhall
home of the Spear-Danes   where that hell's demon
ruled in darkness   with death and thane-grief
through long sorrow-years.   I stopped that murder
so that no other creature   of the kin of Grendel
on this broad earthyard   may boast of that fight—
there were dawn-sounds of victory   vengeance in Heorot
for greed and murder.   I greeted Hrothgar
2010   when I first entered   that ill-fated hall.
Soon that wise one   war-son of Healfdene
was healed from mourning   found hope in my words
made room by his sons   a seat by the gift-throne.
Joy was sung there—seldom have I known
hall-thanes happier   under heaven's arch-vault
such glad-hearted mead-laughter.   Then the good
    folk-queen

weaver of peace-thoughts   walked through the hall
greeted the young ones   gave arm-bracelets
to cheerful warriors   as she went to her seat.
2020   At times in the hall   Hrothgar's daughter-child
offered ale-vessels   to the old counselors—
hall-thanes thanked her   hailed her by name
fair Freawaru   as she fetched the hall-drink,
passed among the benches.   She is promised, I hear,
gold-worthy maiden,   to great Froda's son.
The helm of the Danes   hopes for peace now
bargains with Heathobards   a bride for a truce
buys with his daughter,   his dear girl-child,
a settlement of strife.   Seldom it happens
2030   after shedding of blood   that swords will relax
blood-spears stay idle   though the bride prevail.
Then the young hall-king   Heathobards' leader
and his thanes around him   may think sorrow-thoughts
when he walks with his queen   in the wide meadhall—
a Danish warrior   walks in their company
wears at his side   a shining treasure-sword
gold-hilted warblade   wonder-smith's heirloom
Heathobard weapon   worn to that battle
on that sorrowful day   when their shield-king fell
2040   laid down his life   with his loved ones around him.
Then an old battle-thane   can bear it no more
stares at that Sword-Dane   as he struts past him
remembers with mourning   morning-cold death
grim spear-slaughter   speaks to a young one
reminds him of honor   urges him on
wakening war-thoughts   with words of revenge:
"Do you see, young friend,   the sword on that Dane
that weapon your father   wore to his death
on his last earth-day   that old treasure-sword
2050   he bore to the field   when he fell to Shield-Danes

who won that war-day   after Withergyld lay
sank with his shield   on that sorrowful meadow?
Now this man-child   of a murdering Dane
walks beneath this roof   wearing that battle-blade
that is yours by birth   boasting of murder
proud of that heirloom   pilfered from your kin."
He whispers and urges   whips him with words
with mourning messages   memories of tears
till the queen's hall-thane   is quiet at last
2060   stilled by a swordbite   sleeps forever
stripped of his life—his slayer escapes
slips through the night   to the known woodland.
Then the truce is broken   battle is renewed
oathwords forgotten.   Ingeld remembers
longs for his father—love for his wife
is cooled by that longing   for kin and companions.
I have small hope now   for Heathobards' friendship
peace with the Danes   in the days to come
truce through marriage.

                         I will tell you more
2070   of my fight with Grendel   give you my story
describe clearly   for my king and friend
that hard hand-battle.   When heaven's gem
glided under earth   came an angry guest
evening-grim monster   to that mighty wine-hall
where we all waited   wardens of the night.
He seized Hondscioh   slaughtered him there
our doomed companion—he died quickly
good shield-warrior—Grendel murdered him
crunched him greedily   gulped all of him
2080   crammed into his mouth   that marked doom-warrior.
None the sooner for that   would he stop his murdering
bloody-toothed killer   baleful visitor—
not yet was he ready   to run from that hall

but sure of his strength   he seized my fingers
in his great claw-hand.   A glove hung on him
wide and deep-fingered   woven by elf-smiths
death-bloodied trap   trimmed skillfully
with hides of dragons   hell's murder-work.
He hoped to stuff me   in that huge corpse-bag
2090   cram me inside   carry me from Heorot
one more victim—I waited no longer
stood to greet him   grappled his hand.
It's too long to tell   how I tamed that monster
gave him revenge   with my good handgrip—
in that high meadhall   Hygelac my lord
I memoried your name.   He managed to escape
held to life-breath   for a little more time
left behind him   high beneath the gable
his hand on the wall   wandered in sorrow
2100   to that foul fen-mere   fell to his death.
For that grim battle-rush   the guardian of the Danes
heaped me with heirlooms   horses and armor
many a goldgift   when morning-sun rose
and benches brightened   with banquet in Heorot.
There was song and laughter—the Spear-Danes' king
stretched his memory   for stories of childhood.
At times the old one   touched his harpstrings
strummed the songwood   sang of the past
moments of heartgrief   high victories
2110   remnants of his youth   from reaches of his mind.
At times he brooded   bound by his years
an old sword-warrior   sorrowing for friends
worn with winters   welling with memories
yearning for dead ones   young hearth-fellows.
In that high meadhall   we held to our feasting
drank from treasure-cups   till dark shadow-pall
shoved through the light.   Then sorrow came calling

greedy for thane-blood   Grendel's hell-mother
from her cold moor-cavern   mourning for her son
2120   dead forest-fiend.   That dark-minded she-wolf
avenged her monster-child   vile fen-stalker
killed for her offspring.   It was kind Aeschere
counselor for kings   cold with slaughter-death.
Nor could they find him   when night-shadows paled
bear up his body   for burning on high
lift him to the pyre   beloved companion
for funeral flames.   She fetched his corpse
through the dark forest-track   to her deep water-den.
That was for Hrothgar   the hardest of griefs
2130   sorrows he suffered   through slow winters.
Then the king asked me   for kindness once more
begged me to plunge   through that poisonous water
search for the source   of his soul's misery
pay for that loss.   He promised me treasures.
I swam to the bottom   of that bloodstained pond
dived past hell-demons   to that deep monster-home
where that devil's she-wolf   dragged me inside.
For a while we wrestled   raged through that cavern—
the mere welled with gore   from Grendel's mother
2140   as I carved her head off   in that cavern of death
with a huge giant-sword—from hell's earth-cave
I rose with my life   unready for death.
Then that son of Healfdene   in his hall once more
brought marvelous treasures   to mark my victory.
That king of the Danes   kept his promises—
I lost no reward   for my work that day,
gold for my strength,   for he gave me victory-gifts,
Healfdene's offspring,   to my own desire.
I bring them to you   best of hall-kings
2150   give them with pleasure—my place is in Götland
my life at your service—little do I have

of kin in this earthyard   closer than my lord."
He bore to his guardian   the golden boar-banner
bright-burnished helmet   hand-linked mailcoat
gold-handled sword.   The Geat-champion spoke:
"Hrothgar gave to me   this great treasure-sword
a warleader's weapon—words come with it
borne from the king   with this best of heirlooms.
He said that Heorogar   held it for his own,
2160   lord of the Shield-Danes,   for long battle-years.
Nor would he give it   to his good male-child,
beloved Heoroweard,   though his heart was strong.
Use it as you wish   my young warrior-king!"
Then, as I heard,   to the hall came forth
four war-horses   well-matched and foot-swift
apple-fallow steeds—he served his king there
with kind words and treasures.   So a kinsman should
      do—
no weaving of death-nets   for his dear companion
no sly trickery   treacherous design.
2170   To King Hygelac   helmsman of the Geats
his nephew and friend   was fast in promise
each man to the other   mindful of gifts.
To Hygd the fair one   folk-queen of the Geats
he bore the neck-ring—since that bright feast-day
her breast was enriched   with that royal goldgift.
Three horses he gave her   haltered and saddle-bred.
So he lived in honor   Ecgtheow's son
heartstrong warrior   borne high to acclaim
by pride and mind-strength—not poisoned with ale
2180   did he slay his hearth-friends   with hard murder-blades.
He held to his strength   strongest of them all,
through those long life-days   loaned by the Wielder,
harbored it well.   In the hall of the Geats
as he grew to manhood   no good was thought of him

nor did the Geat-lord   grant him renown
make him treasure-gifts   on mead-benches there—
warriors believed   that his worth was little
no champion there.   But change came to him
courage and war-strength   as he climbed to manhood.
2190 Then King Hygelac   called for his gift—
to the hall was borne   Hrethel's treasure-sword
gold-handled warblade—no Geatish edge-weapon
was stronger in story   more steeped in battle-blood.
He bore that treasure   to Beowulf's hands
gave him seven thousand   of separate domain
hall and gift-stool.   They held together
the kingdom of the Geats   kept it in friendship
the old homeland   though Hygelac's rule
was broader in kind   a king's boundaries.

THE FINAL THIRD of *Beowulf* begins at a time when Beowulf has been ruling the Geats for fifty years, at which point a nameless servant or slave, fleeing punishment for some transgression, stumbles upon a dragon's treasure and steals a cup with which he hopes to buy a pardon. The dragon discovers the theft and begins the destruction that leads to Beowulf's final battle.

The treasure was first buried by nameless nobles, who protected it with a curse referred to near the end of the poem. It was much later unearthed and enjoyed for a time by men who gradually died out, leaving the final survivor who delivers the elegy at the beginning of this section and deposits the treasure in a barrow by the sea, where the dragon discovers it. Ironically, Beowulf dies thinking that the treasure he has won will benefit his people; instead, the Geats burn or bury all of it with Beowulf. As the anonymous messenger indicates towards the end, the old curse will probably punish the Geats since they left much of the treasure undestroyed in the burial mound.

The Geat-Swede conflicts and the fall of Hygelac are presented in a natural if unchronological way at appropriate moments throughout this section of the poem in highly allusive episodes, by the poet himself, by Beowulf, and by the anonymous messenger. In the opening sentence the poet mentions the deaths of Hygelac and his son Heardred, thus bringing together two separate events in a long series summarized as follows:

Three generations of Geats and Swedes are involved in these events. After Haethcyn accidentally kills his older brother Herebeald, King Hrethel of the Geats dies of a broken heart. The Swedes then attack the Geats in Geatish territory at Hreosnabeorh, after which Haethcyn leads a punitive expedition into Swedish territory at Hrefnawudu/Hrefnesholt (alternate names for "Ravenswood"), where Ongentheow, king of the Swedes, kills him and is himself killed by Wulf and Eofor, young Geatish warriors.

The first generation is now gone. Of the Geats, only Hygelac, his young son Heardred, and Beowulf remain. Of the Swedes, there are Ongentheow's sons Onela and Ohthere, and Ohthere's sons Eanmund and Eadgils.

During a pause in the Geat-Swede conflicts, Hygelac leads an expedition up the lower Rhine into the land of Franks and Frisians (including Hugas, Hetware, and Merovingians), where he is killed as he prepares to leave, Beowulf alone escaping. Heardred is now king of the Geats and Ohthere rules the Swedes.

When Ohthere dies, Onela seizes the throne from his nephew and sets in motion a series of conflicts that leave only two principals alive: Eadgils, now king of the Swedes, and Beowulf, now king of the Geats. Fifty years later, Wiglaf, chosen by Beowulf to succeed him, wears the armor of the slain brother of Eadgils, presumably still king of the Swedes, an unfortunate situation.

III

2200   Long afterwards   in lingering years
        after sharp swordswings   sang in anger
        and death found Hygelac   by distant waters—
        after Battle-Swedes came   crossed into Götland
        brought to Heardred   baleful spear-play
        bore him from life   in the land of Weather-Geats
        haled from the gift-throne   Hereric's nephew—
        after Beowulf rose   to rule that kingdom
        fathered the Geats   for fifty winters

learned through the years   lessons of the throne—
2210   once more a monster   moved through the night
a raging flame-dragon   ruled in darkness
fire-grim guardian   of a great treasure-mound
steep stonebarrow—a secret pathway
led to this wealth.   A wandering fugitive
stumbled inside   by the sleeping dragon
stole from the treasure   a studded ale-cup
jeweled gold-vessel.   The jealous goldguard
did not hide his wrath   raged at that theft
by a sneaking runaway.   Soon the Geatfolk
2220   found that his fury   fell upon their land.
Not at all willfully   did that wandering slave
breach that barrow   bear the cup away
but in desperate need   that nameless servant
hiding in heath-slopes   from hateful whiplashing
sorrowful slave-wretch   stumbling for his life
fell into that gloom.   He found quickly
that terror waited there   walled him in fear—
the slumbering serpent   lay still in repose
unwary of his guest   winking jewel-stones
2230   heaped in his coils—one cup was taken
an offering for mercy.

Many were the heirlooms
in that deep earthhouse   old hall-treasures
gathered there in grief   in gone sorrow-days
rings and bracelets   bountiful throne-gifts
left hopelessly   by a last survivor
dear gold-memories.   Death took them all
in times long vanished   victor of men
till one still living   alone with that wealth
lordless hall-warden   could hope no longer
2240   to wield that treasure—time was upon him
boundary of life.   A barrow stood ready

under the bluff-rock   above the waterways
nestled in the cliff   narrow and secret.
He bore those treasures   to the barrow's fold
ring-hoard of warriors   worthy of a king
sealed them in sorrow   and spoke his grief-words:
"Hold you now, Earth   now that heroes are sleeping
these treasures of men.   They were taken from you
by good warrior-friends   gone into silence—
2250   funeral fire-greed   has fetched my people
from their loaned life-days,   led into darkness
bright hall-laughter.   Where are the sword-bearers
quick board-servants   to burnish the ale-cups
vessels of victory?   They have vanished away.
Hard mask-helmets   hand-wrought with gold
shall gleam no longer—good men are sleeping
who should polish them well   for warriors and kings.
This moldering mailcoat   maimed in battle-clash
with bites of edges   over breaking of shields
2260   crumbles in darkness—this death-stained swordvest
can march no longer   linked ring-corselet
by a warrior's side.   No sweet harp-strumming
gathers the songwords   nor the good falcon
swings through the hall   nor the swift battle-steed
clatters in the yard.   Cold death-wardens
have sent into silence   sons of this land."
So the mourning one   mindful of youth-years
one after all of them   wanders alone
through day and night-time   till death's welling
2270   comes to his heart.   The hoard lay open—
the old fire-serpent   found it waiting there
who burns through the air   blasting hall-timbers—
searing hate-creature   soaring through the night
ringed with fire-breath   raging through darkness
torturing earth-dwellers—ever shall he seek

hidden treasure-hoards   heathen gold-chambers
to guard in greed-coils—no good does it bring him.
Three hundred winters   he hoarded his prize
wrapped his rich-gold   in his rocky barrow,
2280 crafty treasure-ward,   till a trembling slave
kindled his anger   carried off a gem-cup
bore it to his lord   begged a settlement
a gift for his life.   That great treasure-mound
was touched by thief-hands—time was granted
to that lucky runaway.   His lord received it
ancient elf's work   ale-cup for a king.
Then that serpent woke   swelled with anger—
he searched the stonework   saw beside the mound
a hostile foot-track   where that hopeless slave
2290 had stolen near to him   stepped past his head.
So may the undoomed   easily survive
sorrow and ruin   he who reaps the favor
of the world's Wielder.   That waking flame-serpent
rushed round his treasure   raged for that thief
who crept past his sleep   swelled him with goldgrief.
Hot with hate-thoughts   he hurtled outside
circled the barrow—he saw no creature
on the wild heathland   hiding from his fury.
At times he shot back   to his bountiful riches
2300 searched for his cup—soon he discovered
that some man-creature   had diminished his hoard
plundered his goldnest.   No patience eased him
as he watched and waited   for waning of that day.
That fearful treasure-guard   fumed with yearning
writhing to ransom   his rich jewel-cup
with flames from the sky.   The sun grew heavy
dragged down the day—the dragon was ready
on his wall by the sea   soared with balefire
fueled by his fury.   The feud had begun,

2310 sorrow for landfolk   which soon would be ended
by their great people-king,   grievously paid for.
That serpent went sailing   spewing flame-murder
blistering meadhalls—mountains of hate-fire
moved through the land—he would leave no creature
alive on the earth   lone night-flyer.
That death-dragon's work   was widely visible
how with vicious vengeance,   violent greed-death,
that winged sky-monster   seared and blasted
the home of the Geats.   To the hoard he dived
2320 dark stonebarrow   as day broke the night.
With great fire-bellows   he flung through the land
bale-flames and ashes—to his barrow he fled
for shelter from sunrise.   Soon all failed him.

To Beowulf was sent   sorrowful tidings
grief-heavy news   that his great meadhall
mightiest of gift-thrones   had melted in flames
cindered by dragon-heat.   That darkest message
was horror to his heart   hardest of fate-strokes.
He thought for a time   he had turned from the Wielder
2330 angered the Shaper   with shameful action
bittered his Maker—his breast was troubled
with dark wonder   deep soul-questions.
The dragon had charred   that champion's kingdom
blasted to ashes   the earth around him
from sea unto sea.   Soon that battle-king
lord of the Geats   would give him answer.
He called for a shield   shaped to his war-needs
a great iron-round   for the Geats' defender
steel life-guardian—he had learned clearly
2340 that no good treewood   could turn back those flames
board against fire-breath.   The border of loan-days
had come for that lord   last of earth-moments

and the dragon as well   doomed to depart
who had lived with treasure   for long centuries.
The old people-king   was too proud for war-troops
had no wish to battle   that wondrous night-flyer
with strong shield-warriors—no serpent's fire-blast
bothered his heartstrength   no hot-searing flames
brought fear to that warrior   who had wagered before
2350   crushed sea-monsters   on the swelling waves
sailed on to Heorot   hall of the Spear-Danes
salvaged Hrothgar   from hell's murderer
grappled with Grendel   and his grim mother-fiend
returned with his life.
                              Not the least of battles
was the meeting of hands   where Hygelac died
king of the Weather-Geats   who came to his death-fight
in the land of Frisians   far from his home—
Hrethel's warrior-son   won his death there
battered by swordswings.   Beowulf escaped
2360   by the strength of his hands   hard grappling-strength—
he hauled to the shore   helmets and corselets
of thirty warriors   from the throng of battle
when he turned towards the sea.   No shield-warriors
of the Hetware race   had reason to boast
of fierce spear-battle—few returned alive
to seek their homeland   after hard swordbites.
Then Ecgtheow's son   only survivor
sailed mourning-sick   to the shore of the Geats.
There Hygd offered him   hoard and kingdom
2370   did not trust her boy   to take the gift-throne
defend it strongly   against slaughtering guests
harbor it from harm   after Hygelac's death-day.
None the sooner for that   could sorrowing Geatfolk
enlist Beowulf   to borrow their throne
take loan of the gift-hall   from beloved Heardred

child-king of Hygelac   chosen by his blood—
he hailed him as lord   held him in friendship
counseled him kindly   till he came to manhood
and the Geats' gift-throne.
                         Grim fugitives
2380   sons of Ohthere   sought his help there—
they fled from Onela   uncle and throne-thief
greatest of sea-kings   Swedes' warrior-lord
who seized the gift-hall   from his good brother-sons.
Heardred paid there   for hosting his friends—
Hygelac's child-king   chose a life-wound
when throne-hungry Onela   Ongentheow's son
followed his nephews   felled young Eanmund
then fled to his homeland   when Heardred lay dead—
left the gift-hall   the Geats' kingdom
2390   in Beowulf's care.   He was kind to his people.
He remembered that day   dark murder-time
gave then to Eadgils   good warrior-help
backed him in sorrow—with shieldmen and horses
he sent that young one   beyond the lake-waters
Ohthere's son   who settled that feud there
mindful of slaughter-days,   stepped to the throne
of the Swedish kingdom.
                         Then King Beowulf
Ecgtheow's son-child   suffered and triumphed
burnishing his name   with bright gift-years
2400   till that fearful twilight   when the fire-dragon soared.
He marched then to battle   one man among twelve
lord of the Geatfolk   to look at that monster.
He had seen before then   the source of that feud
cause of that torment—it came to his hand
precious treasure-cup   through that poor fugitive
who had angered the dragon   entered his gold-barrow—
that thief-slave was now   the thirteenth among them

unwilling guide-servant   guiltily led them
to the sleeping serpent.   He stepped fearfully
2410   to the old earth-hall   ancient stonebarrow
under the seacliff   set into the rock
near the swirling waves.   In its walls were gathered
gems and goldwork.   The guard of that treasure
monstrous fire-warrior   minded his booty
held it under earth—not easily bought
was that glittering gold   not given away.
He sat by the cliffside   keeper of the Geats
hailed his men then   hearth-companions
wished them good luck.   His wavering heart-thoughts
2420   wandered towards death—wyrd was close then
ready to receive   that solemn warrior-king
seek out his soulhoard   sunder it from breath
spirit from body-flesh—the center of his life
would soon be delivered   from its locked flesh-home.
Beowulf spoke   son of Ecgtheow:
"Fierce spear-charges   I fought in my youth
moments of shieldclash—I remember it all.
In my seventh life-year   I was sent from my father
given for training   to that good folk-king
2430   Hrethel of the Geats   who gave me father-love
measured my childhood   mindful of our kinship.
No less was I loved   in those long growth-days
than the sons of that king   kind uncle-friends
Herebeald and Haethcyn   and Hygelac my lord.
The oldest of his sons   by sorrowful chance
slept in a murder-bed   through a sibling's error
when Haethcyn struck   shot from a horn-bow
wounded Herebeald   with a wandering arrow
missed his target   murdered his elder
2440   his blood-loyal brother   with a baleful point.
No payment was made   for that pitiful crime

78

but aching heartwounds   were offered to the king—
no vengeance followed   the fall of that prince.
Same is the sorrow   of a solemn hall-lord
sharp soul-torture   when his son rides hanging
young upon the gallows.   Then he gropes for mercy
sings a horror-song   as his son dangles there
food for the raven—he can find no help
no mercy or revenge   for his mourning heart.
2450   Each morning his mind   measures that deathfall
his son's departure—no patience soothes him
to wait through the years   for young followers
heirs to his treasure   when his only prince
has spoken his last   left him for darkness.
He stares in sorrow   at his son's life-home
the wasted wine-hall   by winds emptied
bereft of bench-joy—riders are sleeping now
silent in their graves—no sound of the harp
warms the meadhall   where men once gathered.
2460   He stays in his bed   sings his heartsongs
no longer does he roam—too roomy they seem
fields and homestead.   So Hrethel in his way
grieved for Herebeald   heavy with sorrow-thoughts
wandering in pain—no way could he find
to bring his slayer   to settle for that death
nor could he hate   Haethcyn his blood-son
or love him still   for that loathsome deed.
His grief was too great   too grim for living—
he gave up his hall-joy   for God's comfort.
2470   To his kin he gave   as a king should do
his land and homestead   when he left this earthyard.
Then trouble began   between Geats and Battle-Swedes
across the lakelands   as they clashed in shield-war
hard killing-times   after Hrethel's deathday
when sons of Ongentheow   sought out the Geats

with angry armies   not eager for peace
held them to battle-play   at Hreosnabeorh's rising
struck against their shields   with sharp blade-edges.
Later in that kind   my kinsmen answered them
2480   took then their blood-pay   as the tale is known
though one paid there   with his precious life-breath
a hard bargain—Haethcyn fell deathwards
king of the Geats   killed in spear-battle.
On the morrow, I heard,   a man took vengeance
with swift sword-anger   slew that king-killer
when Eofor quenched there   Ongentheow's life
mindful of hall-gifts   remembered his lord
did not spare his swordswing   split through the helmet—
the battle-bleak Swede-king   bent down to death.
2490   I repaid lord Hygelac   in proud battle-play
for the treasure he gave   times of the gift-throne,
served him with my sword.   He soon gave me land
homestead and meadhall.   He had no reason
to search among Gifthas   or good Spear-Danes
or the Swedish kingdom   for servants to his throne
to lavish rewards   on a lesser warrior—
always at swordtime   I stood before them all
guided my spearmen   in strong war-clashing
and still I am ready   while this sword endures
2500   this treasured Naegling   that I took from death
on that sorrowful day   when I slew Daeghrefn
killed him with my hands   Hugas' sword-champion—
no time did he have   to take corpse-plunder
fetch breast-corselets   to the Frisian leader
but gave up his life   guardian of the banner
stronghearted warrior.   No sword killed him
but my clenched battle-grip   crushed his bone-house
the springs of his heart.   Now this sword I won there
finest of smith-blades   will fight for that hoard."

2510 Beowulf spoke then   boastwords to fight by
a last venture-speech: "I lived in my youth
through hard war-moments—now here I am ready
battle-weary king   battered with winters
for final glory-time   if that grim hall-burner
will come to meet me   from his mound of gold."
He greeted them then   the Geats around him
good helmet-men   gave them farewell
his final boastwords: "I would bear no sword
no shield or helmet   if my hands could win
2520 settle this fire-fight   with this fuming monster
grapple him deathwards   as with Grendel I did—
but here I expect   hot flame-blasting
life-searing breath—better then for this
are war-shield and corselet.   Not one footstep
will I move from this stone   this smoking barrow.
Wyrd will decide   the way of this meeting
and man's Measurer.   My mind is strong
no more will I boast   of monsters of the past.
Wait in these woods   in your webbed corselets
2530 with shields and ash-spears   to see which of us
will manage to survive   vicious battle-wounds
or kneel here to death.   This is not your fight
nor the measure of anyone   but only myself
to meet this monster   match death with him
reach for his life.   If luck moves with me
I will gather this gold   or give my life here
if cold deathbale   carries me away."
Beowulf rose then   with his round iron-shield
boar-helmet shining   stepped with battle-heart
2540 under the stone-cliff—in his strength he trusted
one against all   no way for a coward!
His tread was still young   after years of warclash
at borders of his land   when boar-banners rushed

81

with a sounding of horns.   He saw by the cliffwall
a stonebarrow standing—a stream broke from it
burst from the wall   bright with fire-flash
blistering the sand—he could step no closer
unburned by that breath   nor bear that dragon-heat
standing so close   as his shield grew hotter.

2550 Then from his breast   bolstered with anger
the lord of the Weather-Geats   loosened a wordblast
stormed stouthearted—under steep graystone
his battle-ready voice   boomed to the mound.
Hate was awakened   the hoard-guardian knew
the sound of that leader—there was little time then
to settle for peace.   From the stone treasure-cave
that monstrous breath-flame   burst in a flash
old anger-fire—the earth trembled.
The strong hall-king   hefted his shield then

2560 sought some relief   from that singeing blast—
that ringed serpent   was ready for combat
greedy for revenge.   The good warrior-king
unsheathed his sword then   swift in its edges
old treasure-blade.   Each of those fighters
warrior and monster   was wary of the other.
Beowulf stood still   with his steep iron-shield
death faced with death   as the dragon coiled then
swelling with fury   simmering with rage.
He burst then roaring   broke from the mound

2570 struck to his fate.   The strong iron-shield
turned back the flames   the fires of that breath
protected that loved one   too little a time
as he found that day   the first war-moment
when wyrd turned from him   took from his hands
luck at battle-play.   He lifted his sword
that son of Ecgtheow   struck at that monster
with the ancient blade—the edge weakened

bit that fiend-bone   in a feebler way
than the king had need of   though he cut strongly
2580 swung with heartstrength.   Then the hoard-guardian
after that swordswing   slithered with anger
spewed his balefire—that searing flame-flash
cindered the meadow.   The mighty Geat-lord
could not boast of victory—his blade failed him there
sharp treasure-steel   betrayed by monster-bone
bit too softly.   Sad came the moment
for that old warrior-king   Ecgtheow's son
to yield ground-plain   give to that monster—
much against his will   he would wander elsewhere
2590 depart from that earthland   as each man will do
give up his loan-days.   Not long after that
monster and man-king   met once again.
The hoardwarden strengthened   with hot breast-roars
the bellows of his breath—in that burning air
embraced by fire-loops   the folk-king suffered.
Not exactly in heaps   did those hand-companions
sons of noblemen   stand close to him
those brave swordswingers   but they bent to the woods
sheltered their lives.   There swelled in one of them
2600 shame-thoughts in his mind.   No man can deny
claims of kinship   if he cares for valor.
Wiglaf his name was   Weohstan's son-child
Aelfhere's kin   keen linden-man
young shield-warrior—he saw his manlord
with blistered battle-mask   blasted by that heat.
He remembered the bounty   from his blood-kin lord
wealthy homestead   of the Waegmundingas
all land and folk-right   his father had owned.
He could bear no shame   brandished his shield,
2610 yellow lindenwood,   lifted on high
his old treasure-sword.   That was Eanmund's weapon

Ohthere's son   sorrowful fugitive
struck down in battle   by brave Weohstan
who gave his armor   to Onela then
shining mask-helmet   steel-meshed mailcoat
ancient wondersword.   Onela returned them
his nephew's war-gear   to Weohstan's hands
found no fault there   no feud between them
though he killed in battle   his blood-brother's son.

2620   He kept that armor   carried it to Götland
stored it safely   till his son was ready
grown up to his shield   shaped for battle-fame.
Among the Geats then   he gave to Wiglaf
that great weapon-prize   as he went from life
forth from the earth.   For the first time now
this strong hearth-soldier   stepped into war-play
fought with his lord   on that fire-black meadow.
His mind did not melt   nor that mighty gift-sword
failed him at need—that fiery gold-serpent

2630   soon discovered that   when they came together.
Wiglaf spoke then   words heart-heavy
shouted with scorn   this shameful message:
"I remember the times   when we took mead-drink
when all of us promised   our proud warrior-king
by the high gift-throne   where he gave us swords
that we'd pay him back   for this bright armor
if ever he needed us,   offer him at spear-time
our helmets and shields.   So did he choose us
picked from his hall-thanes   these proud shieldmen

2640   graced us with gifts   gave me kin-treasures
gathered us to back him   good sword-warriors
eager helmet-men.   Our old gift-lord
meant to manage   this monster-hot battle
alone once again   with his great wonder-strength
armed with a war-name   earned through a lifetime

forged now with deeds.   Now the day has come
when this heartstrong chief   needs help in battle
good sword-wielders.   Let us go quickly
fight beside him   in this fiery business
2650 grim flame-terror.   God knows in me
I'm ready for fire   to feed on my body
cinder me with flames   beside my goldgiver.
It's a poor showing   if we pack our shields
haul them back now   no help to our leader—
we should fell this monster   fight beside our lord
our flame-wounded king.   I can clearly tell you
that it's not old custom   to cringe at this moment
leave him now to suffer   with shame to all of us
burning in this battle.   Now both of us here
2660 will share swordswings   shields and helmets."
He stepped through that hell-reek   hoisted up his
        weapons
brought help to his kinsman   kindled him with words:
"Beloved Beowulf   bear up your heart—
you said in your youth   spoke in yoredays
that you never would allow   while life held to you
the lowering of your name.   Now known through the
        earth
great-hearted Beowulf   bear up your mind-strength
to finish this monster—I will fight beside you."
After those help-words   the angry serpent came
2670 raging gold-monster   glaring with death-eyes
flushed with fire-fury   to flash away the life
of that hateful challenger.   Hard flame-launching
shriveled the shieldwood   seared through mailcoats—
now helpless to endure   that hot serpent-breath
the young hall-thane   hid beside his lord
held to the iron-round   hoping for relief
from those awesome flame-spears.   The old battle-king

85

remembered his glory-name   mightily struck then
with his sharp blade-edge   borne so strongly
2680   that it stuck in that neck.   Naegling burst then
broke upon that bone   Beowulf's trophy-sword
old and battle-hard.   That best of honor-blades
failed him at need   finest of smith-steel
could give him no help.   His hand was too strong
overswung each sword   as stories have told me
struck too forcefully   when he stepped to battle—
wonder-hard weapons   did not work for him.
For the third time then   twisting in hate-coils
that monstrous fire-dragon   mindful of his feud
2690   struck past that shield   with his searing bellows-breath
went straight to Beowulf   bit round his neck
with bitter venom-teeth.   Beowulf stopped then
his life-force draining   in dark blood-welling.
Then, as I heard,   that hall-king's champion
young kin-warrior   came to that monster
with craft and weapon-skill   as his king taught him.
He ducked past the head—hot flame-belching
burned his hand then   as he buried his sword
burnished treasure-blade   in that black snake-belly.
2700   Then that great fire-breath   grew feebler at last
that blistering blast   bellowed more softly
as the blade took hold.   Then Beowulf rose
gathered his mindthoughts   grasped his shortsword
bitter and battle-sharp   broad steel-edges—
the Geat-lord struck   severed the ring-bones.
They felled that fiend   found his life-core
kinsmen together   cut him to hell-death
king and his soldier.   So should a man be
a thane with his lord.   The leader of the Geats
2710   fought his last battle-while   the bourne of his deeds
daytimes of this world.   Then that dragonbite wound

burned into his blood   blistered and swelled there
a monster's deathbite.   Murderous poison
welled within his breast   baleful serpent-gall
pushed towards his heart.   The proud one wandered
slowly by the wall   sat by the barrow-stone
lost in life-thoughts.   He looked upon giants' work
how the stone arches   stout with pillar-strength
the old earth-hall   entered the cliffside.
2720 Then with his hands   that heart-loyal thane
laved him with water,   his beloved blood-king,
youth knelt by age   yearning to comfort
his battle-weary lord   loosened his helmet.
Beowulf spoke then   sick with a life-wound
mortal slaughter-bite.   He saw clearly
that his long life-years   could linger no more
earth's bright moments—all was departing
the number of his days   death immeasurably near:
"Now I would give   to my good son-child
2730 my armor and weapons   if only a land-heir
had been granted to me   to guard my kingdom
prince of my loins.   I have led this people
for fifty long winters.   No folk-king there was
any on this earth   of any neighborland
who dared come to me   with dark battle-rush
goad me with his spears.   In this good homeland
I lived through time-fate   looked to my kingdom
sought no treachery   swore no oath-lies
warped anger-words.   For all these things
2740 sick with life-wound   I sing in my heart.
The Shaper of men   cannot shame my going
with murder-bale of kinsmen   at the moment of silence
when life darkens.   Leave me to rest here
go to that goldhoard   under gray cliffrock,
beloved Wiglaf,   now the worm lies cooling

sleepened by swords   stripped of his treasure.
Hurry, my warrior,   help me to see
this serpent's wealth-hoard   shining gold-collars
bright wonder-gems—bear them before me
to ease my heartbane   help me to leave
this life and people   that I long have held."
Charged with those words   Weohstan's son-child
obeyed his beloved   life-weary kinsman
stepped through the stench   of stilled dragon-breath
entered the rock-vault   of that ancient barrow.
Enclosed there by pillars   piles of heirlooms
glinted in the gloom   gleaming treasure-heaps
glittering gemstones   by the gray rockwork
wonders by the walls   in that worm's gold-den
the old dawn-flyer's   ancient wine-vessels
rich silver-cups   bereft of polishers
stripped of ornament.   There were swordstruck helmets
old and rust-laden   arm-bracelets tarnishing
curiously twisted.   A king's treasure-mound
gold upon the ground   will grab at the minds
of all hall-warriors   hidden though it be.
High above the hoard   like a hovering glow-lamp
hung a golden banner   greatest of handworks
laced with limbcraft—light shone from it
gleamed through the darkness   a guide for his eyes
to stare at wonders.   Of that serpent's coil
no trace could be seen—swords had removed him.
Then, as I heard,   that hoard was plundered
smith-wonders gathered   by a sorrowing warrior
who piled in his arms   plates and jewel-cups
to his own liking   and the old gold-banner
brightest of standards.   Biting steel-edges
fire-hardened swordblades   freed that treasure-trove
quenched the hate-fire   hot terror-breath

2750

2760

2770

2780 of that lone mound-miser   who measured the land
belching with flame-waves   burning through the night
searing the darkness   till he died of murder.
Wiglaf hurried then   weighted with that bounty
trembling to learn   if his beloved shield-king
was breathing life-breath   as he last saw him
lord of the Weather-Geats   waiting for treasures
sick with blood-bane   bordered in darkness.
Wrapped in those riches   he rushed to his lord
stricken bounty-king   seared and wound-weary
2790 at the end of life.   He laved him again
wakened him with water   till words came pressing
broke through his breast.   The battle-king spoke then
gazed at the goldworks   that great treasure-pile:
"For these fine war-trophies   I finally must say
thanks to the Wielder   Wonder-King of all
our glorious Shaper   for such gold and gemstones
that I now may leave   to my beloved Geatfolk
at this last death-moment   darkening of light.
Now that I've bought   this bright treasure-mound
2800 with my old lifeblood   look to my kingdom
the needs of my Geats—I must now leave you.
Tell my battle-friends   to build me a mound
high by the balefire   on the headland's point.
It will signal my name   to sons of this nation
tower to the sky   on tall Hronesnaess
so that sea-travelers   in time will call it
Beowulf's barrow   as they beat through the swells
sail their prow-ships   on the pounding waves."
He removed from his throat   a marvelous neck-ring
2810 gold-gleaming collar   gave it to his thane,
young spear-warrior,   yielded his armor
helmet and mailcoat   hailed him farewell:
"You are the last   of our beloved kinsmen

the Waegmunding clan.   Wyrd has guided
all of my family   to fate's shadowland
my fine companions—I will follow them now."
Those words were the last   of that long-loved king
his final heart-thoughts   for the hot balefire
bone-cracking flames—from his breast at last
2820 his soul went seeking   safety in praise.
Young Wiglaf then   yearned for his master
wept within his mind   as he watched the old one
loved throne-warden   lay down his earthyears
moments of his life.   The monster sprawled there
uncoiled earthdragon   cut down from flight
ended by swordswings.   That old death-flyer
no longer wielded   his wealthy ringhoard
but steel blade-edges   stopped his life-fire
hard and battle-sharp   smith-hammer's leaving.
2830 That soaring night-flyer   stilled by murder-wounds
fell to the earth   near that fire-kept treasure.
No longer at sunset   did he sail with hate-flames
roaming the night-dark   raging for his cup
scorching the skyways   but he sank at last
hushed by the swordwork   of heartstrong warriors.
Few good battle-men   bold though they be
strongest in warfare   swordmen to be feared
reckless in life-dare   ready for deathday
would stand against the blast   of that searing heat-breath
2840 touch with their hands   the tiniest of gems
if they found waiting there   a waking moundguard
coiled in his barrow.   Beowulf exchanged
those lordly treasures   for his life's boundary—
king and enemy   earned the end there
of their loaned earth-days.
                                          Not long from then
those safe war-watchers   stole from the woods

cowardly trust-breakers   ten sword-shirkers
who dared not earlier   enter with their shields
in that hard moment   of their manlord's need.
2850 They came with their swords   shamed war-weapons
aching with silence   where the old one lay.
They looked then at Wiglaf   who watched hopelessly,
one man alone   by his lord's shoulder,
bathed him with water—no breath came to him.
No way could he find   no wishful begging
to lengthen the life   of that loved gift-king
nor change the Measurer's   moment of release—
the judgment of God   would guide the destiny
of every man-creature   as it always does.
2860 Then grim welcome-words   welled in the heart
of that young shieldman   for those shameful wretches.
Wiglaf spoke then   Weohstan's offspring
grief-heavy warrior   glared at unloved ones:
"That he may say   who will speak the truth
that this good manlord   who made you such gifts
rich war-trappings   that you wear this moment,
by bright ale-benches   bettered you with swords
burnished shield-boards   byrnies and helmets
from lord to his thanes,   lent you the finest
2870 of all steel-swords   smith-wrought with care
that he then utterly   all that battle-gear
entirely wasted   in the time of his need.
That lonesome folk-king   could find no cause
to boast of his war-thanes   but the broad Wielder
Worldshaper granted   that our great manlord
alone with his sword   served that monster.
Little of life-help   could I lend him then
give him at battle   but I gathered my courage
over my war-strength   to aid my kinsman.
2880 Always the weaker   was that old night-flyer

when I struck him below—slackened fire-breath
flamed from his head.   Too few warriors
crowded around him   courage was not great.
Now shall treasure-gifts   the taking of swords
all homeland joys   in the halls of your kinsmen
all happiness cease.   You will sorrowfully wander
stripped of landrights   beloved homesteads
alone in your exile   when other battle-thanes
learn of your failure   your flight to the woods
2890   dragging your life-shields.   Death will be better
for each one of you   than a wasted life."
He sent the news then   a solemn messenger
up by the cliff-edge   where the curious Geats
all morning-long   mourningly waited
wondering in silence   what was shaped for their lord—
the end of his life   or unlikely return
of their loved hall-king.   He lacked no doom-words
that ready news-speaker   who rode to the headland
but called out clearly   to the crowd waiting there:
2900   "Now is the goldking   of the Geatish landfolk
friendlord to us all   fast in his death-sleep
dwelling in slaughter-rest   through that serpent's teeth.
Unflaming lies now   that lone night-scorcher
sickened by shortsword.   With sharp Naegling
our war-crafty leader   could work no life-wound
on that venomous head.   Hard by Beowulf
Wiglaf waits for us   Weohstan's blood-son
young war-champion   watching over death
holds with sorrow-thoughts   a silent head-guard
2910   by monster and lord.   We will live to see
dark slaughter-days   when the death of our king
is widely heralded   over wave-rolling seas
to Franks and Frisians.   That feud was started
hard against Hugas   when Hygelac went forth

92

sailing with float-troops   to Frisian territory
where the swordstrong Hetware   humbled him in battle
gained victory there   with greater force-fighting
till that best of spear-kings   bent down to death
fell among foot-troops—no fine gold-plunder
2920 he brought to our hall.   Since that heavy slaughter-day
no stern Merovingians   have sent us peace-tokens.
Nor will Battle-Swedes   bear us good tidings
wish us good will   but it's widely known
that stout Ongentheow   struck to the life-core
of Haethcyn Hrethling   at Hrefnawudu's edge
when eager for power   the proud Geat-force
went seeking with spears   the Swedish thane-warriors.
Soon the old one   Ohthere's father
taught them battle-lore   turned back their forces
2930 cut down their leader   recaptured his wife
grand throne-lady   of her gold bereft
Onela's and Ohthere's   old queen-mother—
followed them then   fugitive invaders
till they sheltered at last   that sorrowful evening
in dark Hrefnesholt   heavy with life-loss.
He laughed at that army   the leavings of swords
wearied by their wounds.   Great woes he promised
those wretched survivors   right through the night
said that at dawning   with swords' edges
2940 he would hew them down   hang them on gallows-trees
for the pleasure of birds.   At breaking of day
the sorrowful Geatmen   were consoled once more
when they heard Hygelac's   horn-song of challenge
heartlift for survivors   when revenge came calling,
a band of sword-thanes   bearing through the woods.
Great were the bloodtracks   of Geats and Swedes there
loud shield-clashing   leapt through the trees
as two great armies   tried for victory.

Then the old warrior   wise in spearways
2950   turned back his people   took them to shelter,
lord Ongentheow   leading them away—
he had learned of Hygelac's   hard warrior-ways
that proud one's swordcraft—he put no trust
in open battle-play   with the best of Geats
guarded his hoardwealth   held there in safety
his wife and children—he went to ground then
shielded by earthwall.   Then the old Swede-lord
was hounded once more—Hygelac's boar-banner
sailed above them   streamed through the morning
2960   when Geats came running   rushed the shieldwall.
Then brave Ongentheow   battle-wise Swede-king
was brought down to earth   by edges of swords—
at last he consented   to live or die there
by Eofor's judgment.   In earlier fighting
Wulf Wonreding   wielded his sword
with such blade-biting   that blood sprang in streams
from that gray hairline.   Still game for fighting
the old Swede-lord   swung back at him
repaid that wound   with a worse exchange
2970   when that proud folk-king   fought for his life.
Nor could that swordman   shield-son of Wonred
give the old one   a good counterblow
for the Swedish war-king   sheared through his helmet
stained him with blood   till he bowed at last
fell down to earth.   Yet fate was not ready—
Wulf soon recovered   though cut to the bone.
Then his helpful blood-brother   Hygelac's thane
struck with his sword   to save his kinsman
swung his treasure-blade   sliced to the grayhead
2980   through the king's helmet—he crumbled then
Swedefolk's guardian   slipped down from life.
No lack of blade-friends   broke through the shieldwall

bound Wulf in wrappings   when warfare allowed them
when they ruled the field   in the falling of light.
Then Eofor stripped there   the slain warrior-king
took from Ongentheow   his iron corselet
hilted treasure-sword   tall mask-helmet
bright war-trappings   bore them to Hygelac
who kept all of it   clearly promised him
2990 ample rewards then   afterwards gave them.
The lord of the Geats   great Hrethel's son
called to the gift-throne   those good thane-brothers
gave Wulf and Eofor   wondrous treasure-gifts
gave each to hold   a hundred thousand
of land and goldrings—no good hall-thane
could envy that treasure   earned with heartstrength—
and to Eofor gave   his only daughter-child
a princess for his home   and a pledge of favor.
For that we will pay   those proud survivors
3000 for slaughter of kin   killed in their homeland
when young Swede-warriors   strike once again
learn that Beowulf   our beloved warleader
lies lifeless now   his last breath-moment
vanished into time   a tale for mead-benches
songs for a king   who crushed hell-monsters
stepped up to a throne   served his people there
held high his promise.   Now haste will be best
that we go to find him   guide him at last
from that fire-black field   where he fell deathwards
3010 to his final bedrest.   Those fine gold-treasures
will melt with his heart   that mighty dragon-hoard
shall all go with him   grimly purchased
with his own lifeblood—for the last time now
he has paid for goldrings.   Pyre-flames shall eat them
flame-roof shall thatch them   no thane shall wear them
treasures so dear   no dressed hall-maidens

shall wear on their bosoms   wound-gold necklaces
but grief will adorn them   of gold-love bereft
as they wander in exile   through alien domains
3020 now that our lord   has laid down his laughter
songs and hall-joys.   Now spears will be lifted
grim and morning-cold   gripped in anguish
with frost-numbing hands.   No harp's sweet sounding
will waken bench-warriors   but the black-gleaming raven
circling with fate   will say many things
describe to the eagle   ample corpse-banquets
how he shared with the wolf   wondrous
    slaughter-meals."
So that grim messenger   gave his report
his unfrivolous news   nor did he lie much
3030 in words or warnings.   Warriors all rose
uneagerly shuffled   under Earnanaess
lagging with sorrow   to look upon death.
They found on the sand   their soulless gift-lord
still and wordless there   who served and ruled them
for fifty winters—the final life-day
had come for the good one—the Geats' hall-master
dear warrior-king   died a wonder-death.
There they discovered   that cooling fire-snake
stretched upon the earth,   seething no more
3040 with foul flame-death   flying no longer
with burning bellows,   blackened with death.
Fifty long feet   was his full length-measure
stretched on the fire-field.   He flew in hate-joy
seared through the nights   then soared at daybreak
to his grayrock den—now death stilled him
ended his slumber   in that stony barrow.
By him were heaped   bracelets and gem-cups
etched gold-dishes   great treasure-swords
darkened with rust   from their deep earth-home

3050 a thousand winters   walled against light.
Those ancient heirlooms   earned much curse-power
old gold-treasure   gripped in a spell—
no one might touch them   those nameless stone-riches
no good or bad man   unless God himself
the great Glory-King   might give to someone
to open that hoard   that heap of treasures,
a certain warrior   as seemed meet to him.
They found no happiness   who first buried there
riches in the ground—again it was hidden
3060 by an only survivor   till an angered serpent
slaughtered for a cup   till swords calmed him
shoved him deathwards.   Strange are the ways
how the king of a country   will come to the end
of his loaned life-span   when at last he vanishes
gone from the meadhall   his gold and his kin.
So it was with Beowulf   when he bore his shield
to that roaring night-flyer.   He could not foretell
how his great throne-days   would gutter to darkness.
Those ancient sorcerers   swore a greed-spell
3070 baneful warriors   who buried their treasure
so that all plunderers   would be punished with misery
confined in an idol-grove   fast in hell-bonds
scourged with torture   who tread on that ground—
unless for gold-need   he was granted in fee
the gold-owner's favor   with full pardon.
Wiglaf spoke then   son of Weohstan:
"Oft shall warriors   through the will of one
come to heartgrief   heavy mind-sorrow.
Our eldest wisemen   could not win with speech
3080 convince with their words   the ward of our kingdom
to give to destiny   that goldhoard's keeper
leave him coiled there   where he long had slumbered
wrapped in that barrow   till the world's end-day.

He held to his name—the hoard is opened
grimly purchased—too great was that fate
that brought our hall-king   to that baleful place.
I stepped inside there   saw all around me
the wealth of that hoard   walled by cliffrock—
the price for that entrance   was paid heavily
3090 by monster and man.   From that mound I gathered
grabbed with my hands   a great treasure-pile
bright gold and gemstones   bore them out then
to my suffering king.   Still quick I found him
proud of his winnings   wavering in thought.
Old and weakening   he offered you greetings
asked that you build   in honor of his deeds
over the balefire   an arching barrow-mound
high above the sea   hailing his name there
greatest of warriors   through this wide earthyard
3100 landlord of our hearts   homestead and glory.
Now comes the time   to tame this gold-curse
open and plunder   that ancient treasure-pile
wonders under wall-stone—the way is clear now,
come to gaze at it   curious jewel-cups
rings and broad-gold.   Let the bier be lifted
raised and flame-ready   for ritual of death.
We will fetch our hall-lord   to that final gift-throne
our beloved people-king   where he long shall rest
fast in the Wielder's   wonderful embrace."
3110 He sent word then   that son of Weohstan
man of command now   to many a homestead
Geats from everywhere   to gather up bale-wood
fetch from afar   funeral branch-logs
for that final departure: "Now the fire shall rise
dark flames roaring   with our dear gift-lord
who held against war-hail   hard iron-showers
when storms of arrows   angrily impelled

shot over shieldwall   when shafts of ash-wood
straight with feather-gear   followed the arrowheads."
3120   Then that young warrior   Weohstan's offspring
picked from his men   proud warrior-thanes
seven of his best   strong Geat-champions
went one of eight   under that rock-roof
best of shield-bearers—one bore in his hand
a pitch-bright pinetorch   pushed back the darkness.
There was no dawdling   by that dragon's greed-hoard
when they found unguarded   such gold and gemstones
wondrous treasures   waiting in that hall
lying about them—little did they wait
3130   but hurried to gather   haul to daylight
those dark wonderworks.   The dragon they shoved
over the cliffwall   into cold wave-water
let the sea embrace   that shepherd of wealth.
Then a wagon was loaded   with wound goldrings
numberless bracelets   borne beside the warrior
whose heart paid for them   to Hronesnaess point.
They raised skyward   ready for their king
a pyre on that point   for their proud warleader
hung it with helmets   hard shield-bosses
3140   bright mesh-corselets   as he bade them do.
They laid in the middle   their beloved gift-friend
lifted with heartgrief   the helm of their land.
On the cliff they kindled   a king's balefire
wavering death-flames—woodsmoke mounted
rose up darkly   over roaring pitch-flames
wailing to the sky.   The wind lay low
till that fire had broken   the body's flesh-cover
conquering that heart.   With heavy memories
they mourned their mind-care   their manlord's going.
3150   By the embers of grief   an old Geat-woman
with bound mourning-hair   bowed down by years

sang a sorrow-song   said to the heavens
that she dreaded from then   days of misery
dark war-slaughter   wailing and death-tears
heart-weary wandering.   Heaven took the smoke.
Then that king's followers   formed a mound there
a huge barrow-grave   high and broad-based
sighted from afar   by foam-borne sailors.
They timbered on top   in ten workdays
3160   a towering beacon   on that balefire's leavings
wrapped it with a wall   as worthiest craftsmen
cleverest artisans   could cause to be built.
In that barrow they placed   bracelets and gems
ancient smith-work   of old nameless ones
brought from the rock-den—each beaker and dish
went back to the earth   bright gold and meadcups
stored once again   where they still lie waiting
as useless to man   as they ever had been.
Around the barrow-base   rode the lost ones
3170   twelve good spearmen   circled the mound
mourned their hall-lord   hailed their good king
spoke of his courage   sang their word-songs
praised his earlship   and his proud throne-years
as good men should   when their shieldman has gone.
A good wine-lord   needs words of praise
love from his people   when he leaves this earth
when breath is borne   from his body at last.
So the Geats went grieving   gathered by the mound.
Hearth-companions   praised their lost one
3180   named him the ablest   of all world-kings
mildest of men   and most compassionate
most lithe to his people   most loving of praise.

Genealogies

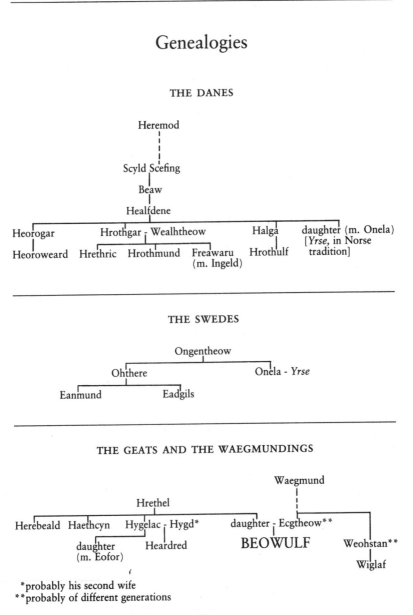

THE DANES

Heremod

Scyld Scefing

Beaw

Healfdene

Heorogar — Hrothgar - Wealhtheow — Halga — daughter (m. Onela) [*Yrse*, in Norse tradition]

Heoroweard — Hrethric — Hrothmund — Freawaru (m. Ingeld) — Hrothulf

THE SWEDES

Ongentheow

Ohthere — Onela - *Yrse*

Eanmund — Eadgils

THE GEATS AND THE WAEGMUNDINGS

Waegmund

Hrethel

Herebeald — Haethcyn — Hygelac - Hygd* — daughter - Ecgtheow** — Weohstan**

daughter (m. Eofor) — Heardred — BEOWULF — Wiglaf

*probably his second wife
**probably of different generations

101

Selected Proper Names

Members of the royal families, other important names, and names appearing more than once

AESCHERE: Hrothgar's beloved counselor, carried away by Grendel's mother.

BEAW: Son of Scyld Scefing; father of Healfdene.

BEOWULF: Hero of the poem; both a Waegmunding and a Geat by birth (see genealogies).

BRECA: Beowulf's companion in a daring youthful swimming contest described by both Unferth and Beowulf.

CAIN: Biblical son of Adam and slayer of his brother, Abel; begetter of monsters.

DAEGHREFN: A warrior of the Hugas killed by Beowulf during Hygelac's fatal expedition to the Rhine; Beowulf apparently took his sword, Naegling, and used it until his death day.

EADGILS: Swedish prince, son of Ohthere; later Swedish king.

EANMUND: Brother of Eadgils; slain by Wiglaf's father, Weohstan, who served Eanmund's uncle, Onela, for a time.

ECGLAF: Father of Unferth.

ECGTHEOW: Beowulf's father, a Waegmunding who married Hygelac's sister.

EOFOR: Geatish warrior; slayer of Ongentheow; brother of Wulf.

FINN: Frisian king, married to the Danish princess Hildeburh; initiated the Battle of Finnsburuh when Hildeburh's brother Hnaef came to his court for a visit; later killed by Hengest.

103

FITELA: In *Beowulf*, nephew of Sigemund the dragon slayer.

FRANKS: Prominent West Germanic tribe.

FREAWARU: Hrothgar's daughter; betrothed to Ingeld, prince of the Heathobards.

FRISIANS: Prominent West Germanic tribe.

FRODA: King of the Heathobards; father of Ingeld.

GRENDEL: Anthropomorphic monster who ravaged Heorot for twelve years; killed by Beowulf and avenged by GRENDEL'S MOTHER, also killed by Beowulf. Both were descendants of Cain by way of Noah's son Ham, according to early medieval tradition.

HAERETH: Father of Hygd.

HAETHCYN: Elder brother of Hygelac; accidentally killed his brother Herebeald with an arrow, causing his father, Hrethel, to die of grief.

HALGA: Younger brother of Hrothgar; father of Hrothulf; dead before Beowulf's arrival at Heorot.

HEALFDENE: Father of Hrothgar; son of Beaw.

HEARDRED: Son of Hygelac; a young boy when Hygelac was killed, became king of the Geats under Beowulf's protection; was later killed for harboring Swedish fugitives Eanmund and Eadgils.

HEATHOBARDS: Germanic tribe to which Ingeld belonged.

HEMMING: Kinsman of Offa.

HENGEST: Leader of the Danes after Hnaef's death at the Battle of Finnsburuh.

HEOROGAR: Elder brother of Hrothgar; dead before Beowulf's arrival at Heorot.

HEOROT: Splendid meadhall built by Hrothgar and ravaged by Grendel.

HEOROWEARD: Son of Hrothgar's elder brother, Heorogar.

HEREBEALD: Eldest son of Hrethel; older brother of Hygelac; accidentally killed by Haethcyn, his younger brother.

HEREMOD: Early Danish king who turned against his people and died without an heir, leaving the Danes kingless until the arrival of Scyld Scefing.

HETWARE: Frankish people on the lower Rhine; engaged in battle against Hygelac.

HNAEF: Hildeburh's brother, slain by his brother-in-law Finn.

HOC: Danish king; father of Hnaef and Hildeburh.

HONDSCIOH: Geatish warrior devoured by Grendel in Heorot.

HREFNAWUDU/HREFNESHOLT: (alternate names meaning "Ravens-wood") ; forest in Sweden, scene of a Geat-Swede battle.

HREOSNABEORH: Hill in Götland; scene of a Geat-Swede battle.

HRETHEL: Danish king; father of Hygelac.

HRETHRIC: Young son of Hrothgar and Wealhtheow.

HRONESNAESS: Headland in Götland; site of Beowulf's barrow.

HROTHGAR: Danish king; builder of Heorot.

HROTHMUND: Young son of Hrothgar and Wealhtheow.

HROTHULF: Son of Halga.

HRUNTING: Unferth's sword, loaned to Beowulf for his fight with Grendel's mother.

HUGAS: A Frankish people.

HYGD: Wife of Hygelac.

HYGELAC: King of the Geats; uncle of Beowulf.

INGELD: Heathobard prince; according to Beowulf, betrothed to Hrothgar's daughter, Freawaru.

NAEGLING: Beowulf's sword in later life; probably taken from Daeghrefn.

OFFA: King of the Continental Angles in the fourth century; king of Mercia (English Midlands) in the eighth century.

OHTHERE: Son of Ongentheow.

ONELA: Son of Ongentheow; usurper of Swedish throne.

ONGENTHEOW: Swedish king; killed by Wulf and Eofor in battle.

SCYLD SCEFING: Legendary Danish king who arrived mysteriously as a child in a drifting boat and began a new dynasty, apparently many years after the death of Heremod.

SIGEMUND: In *Beowulf*, son of Waels and a famous dragon slayer.

UNFERTH: Hrothgar's *thyle;* challenger of Beowulf in a duel of words; a difficult character to understand (see my comments in the translation following line 498.)

WAEGMUNDINGS: Family to which Ecgtheow, Beowulf, Weohstan, and Wiglaf belong.

WAELS: In *Beowulf,* father of Sigemund (cf. Völsungs in Norse tradition).

WEALHTHEOW: Hrothgar's queen.

WELAND: Legendary Germanic smith.

WEOHSTAN: Wiglaf's father, a Waegmunding who served the Swedish king Onela for a time and killed Eanmund, Onela's nephew.

WIGLAF: Weohstan's son; young warrior who helps Beowulf kill the dragon; Beowulf's kinsman (a Waegmunding) and successor.

WULF: Eofor's brother, who badly wounded Ongentheow before Eofor killed him.

WULFGAR: Hrothgar's herald, who welcomed Beowulf and his men to Heorot.

YRSE: Name of Hrothgar's sister; not found in *Beowulf;* suggested by Kemp Malone to fill an obvious lacuna in the manuscript.

Suggested Readings

1. GENERAL

Beowulf and Its Analogues, edited and translated by G. N. Garmonsway and Jacqueline Simpson, including "Archaeology and *Beowulf*" by Hilda Ellis Davidson (J. M. Dent & Sons, 1968). Exhaustive collection of just what the title indicates, including a prose translation of the poem by the editors. Useful information on all families and tribes in *Beowulf* as well as the monsters; enlightening essay on pertinent archaeological finds with excellent photographs.

Beowulf: Reproduced in Facsimile, etc., with transliteration and notes by Julius Zupitza; second edition by Norman Davis with improved reproduction, published for the Early English Text Society (Oxford University Press, 1959). For the specialist or adventurous amateur; reading a facsimile of the manuscript is a wonderful experience for anyone with a basic knowledge of Old English.

Adrien Bonjour, *The Digressions in Beowulf,* Medium Aevum Monograph V (Basil Blackwell, 1965). A very perceptive discussion of the "digressions" in *Beowulf,* primarily dealing with their artistic justification.

Arthur G. Brodeur, *The Art of Beowulf* (University of California Press, 1959). A marvelous, affectionate examination of virtually all aspects of the poem by a fine scholar; required reading for students of *Beowulf.*

R. W. Chambers, *Beowulf: An Introduction to the Poem with a Discussion of the Stories of Offa and Finn,* third edition by C. L. Wrenn

(Cambridge University Press, 1958). Originally published in 1921, this is the *Beowulf* student's bible, a vast accumulation of learning by two fine scholars examining historical and nonhistorical elements as well as the origin, date, and structure of the poem, with copious documentation. Nicely complemented by Brodeur's book.

Edward B. Irving, Jr., *An Introduction to Beowulf* (Prentice-Hall, 1969). One hundred pages introducing the beginner to the background and offering a "critical run-through" of the poem.

Edward B. Irving, Jr., *A Reading of Beowulf* (Yale University Press, 1968). An engrossing presentation of one well-informed scholar's reaction to the poem; readable and stimulating.

Kenneth Sisam, *The Structure of Beowulf* (Oxford University Press, 1965). An examination of the poem's structure as it would have been perceived by an Anglo-Saxon audience a thousand years ago, justifying the poem's effective diversity of mood; followed by other observations and notes by this deeply learned and meditative scholar. An interesting complement to Whitelock's *Audience* (see below), some features of which Sisam discusses.

J. R. R. Tolkien, "*Beowulf:* The Monsters and the Critics," from *Proceedings of the British Academy,* vol. 22 (Oxford University Press, 1936). Also available in *An Anthology of Beowulf Criticism,* edited by Lewis E. Nicholson (University of Notre Dame Press, 1963), and *The Beowulf Poet,* edited by Donald K. Fry (Prentice-Hall, 1968). See the beginning of my introduction for the importance of this delightful, witty lecture.

Dorothy Whitelock, *The Audience of Beowulf* (Oxford University Press, 1951). A collection of three lectures by a great scholar, always keeping in mind Anglo-Saxon contemporaries of the *Beowulf* poet and using things known to and experienced by them to explain the poet's methods of composition; includes an intelligent discussion of the possible dates of the poem's composition. Like Sisam's book (see above), which it usefully complements, recommended for its brevity and wisdom.

2. EDITIONS

Beowulf and the Fight at Finnsburg, edited by Frederick Klaeber, third edition, D. C. Heath, 1950. Even for those not well trained in Old English, this edition, greatest of them all, is worth studying if only for its fine introductory material and exhaustive textual notes.

Beowulf and the Finnsburg Fragment, edited by C. L. Wrenn, revised edition, 1958; fully revised in 1973 by W. F. Bolton (all editions, George C. Harrap and Company). A briefer (to some "more accessible") edition than Klaeber's, very authoritative. Bolton's textual notes at page foot are attractive.

3. ANGLO-SAXON HISTORY

Frank M. Stenton, *Anglo-Saxon England,* third edition, completed by Doris Mary Stenton (Oxford University Press, 1971). The greatest of all histories of Anglo-Saxon England, some seven hundred pages of profound erudition with an excellent foldout map. Not for the beginner.

Dorothy Whitelock, *The Beginnings of English Society,* vol. 2 in the Pelican History of England (Penguin Books, 1952). In less than 250 pages this superb scholar has examined every aspect of Anglo-Saxon civilization, working consistently with primary sources and setting forth in captivating detail and graceful prose the evidence for her conclusions. This is *the* book for nonspecialist readers.

4. OLD ENGLISH LANGUAGE AND LITERATURE

It is possible for an interested and disciplined reader to learn Old English well enough to move on to Klaeber's or Wrenn's edition of *Beowulf* without benefit of a teacher. Readers unable or unwilling to attend a class in Old English should obtain a copy of the third edition of *Bright's Old English Grammar and Reader,* edited by Frederic G. Cassidy and Richard N. Ringler (second, corrected printing, Holt, Rinehart & Winston, 1974). This book is skillfully designed to prepare the reader for the good selections of prose and poetry that follow the introductory chapters on pronunciation and grammar. Photographs of several Old English manuscript folios, a thorough introduction to all aspects of Old English poetry, and detailed maps inside the front and back covers help to make this the best of all Old English grammar/readers.